The Untraining of a Sea Priestess

....

*A Practical Journey
to Connect with
Cosmic Water Wisdom*

The Untraining of a Sea Priestess

....

*A Practical Journey
to Connect with
Cosmic Water Wisdom*

STEPHANIE LEON NEAL~

**TURNING
STONE
PRESS**

Copyright © 2017
by Stephanie Leon Neal

All rights reserved, including the right to reproduce this
work in any form whatsoever, without permission
in writing from the publisher, except for brief passages
used in connection with a review.

Cover design by Frame25 Productions
Cover art by Arlo Magicman c/o Shutterstock.com
Author photo by Christina Dianne Photography
Interior design by Howie Severson

Turning Stone Press
8301 Broadway St., Ste. 219
San Antonio TX, 78209
turningstonepress.com

Library of Congress Control Number
available upon request

ISBN 978-1-61852-115-6

10 9 8 7 6 5 4 3 2 1

Printed in the United States of America

I would like to pour my gratitude over my husband Rev. Mike Neal, HP, for he has been my ship and rudder since 1969. He has steadfastly given me love comparable to no other thing on earth.

Contents

Introduction	ix
Chapter 1: Untangle	1
Chapter 2: Release: There Goes a Frog	15
Chapter 3: Dreaming	27
Chapter 4: Running with the Moon	47
Chapter 5: Some Reasons Why We Disconnect	63
Chapter 6: Move	75
Chapter 7: Poisoned Waters	91
Chapter 8: Fly!	101
Chapter 9: Divination	109
Chapter 10: Who Is a Sea Priestess?	125
Chapter 11: The Cracked Water Pot	141
Chapter 12: Falling into the Others	145
Chapter 13: The Unteacher	155
Chapter 14: Some Water Associations	167
Chapter 15: Sea Priestess Initiation	179

Introduction

Welcome to the Deep Waters of the Sea Priestess. Warning! If you are reading these lessons for just the purpose of accumulating more knowledge, be careful, because you may fall into the sea and become more than you could have ever imagined. Consider each word a soothing, fragrant sea balm, a letter given just for you; every word spoken, just for your ears. It takes courage to allow yourself, maybe for the first time in your life, to be touched and comforted. It may have been a very long time since you were uplifted or validated in any fashion. Your soul will begin to speak this very moment, saying, "Now is the time to reclaim my purposes and joy!"

Every lesson is a living love letter to you, because indeed you are loved beyond measure. My desire is that, by the end of these lessons, you will stand in your full glory, because the world is waiting for you. The seas are waiting for you. That is a fact! You are not here by accident, you are here by design—your design. Becoming a Sea Priestess is incredibly reachable if you have a pure, selfless heart and pure motives; that's all that is needed to take this journey across the wide seas.

Becoming a Sea Priestess means you will have done extensive shadow and stream cycle work, while focusing on the positive side of issues. You will be balanced to the point that there is no balance, because the two become one. It is important to focus on what you desire, not what you don't desire or hope to obtain someday, because someday will never come. Sea Priestesses and Priests are pioneers and philosophers of a different kind. We wait for no hero or person or thing that is perceived to be more than us. We do not believe we are not enough or you are not enough. Instead we know we are more than enough and so are you. And because we know we are the heroes, there is no more waiting.

If we focus only on the negative aspect of a problem or try to find the "root" of a shadow, then we gain nothing, except spending more time in shadow. If you want to spiritually heal, at soul level, and live a bombastic life, then you will. It is all up to you; everything has always been up to you.

Sea Priestess Path

As you dive into these lessons, know you are entering another world, a world that has been waiting for you for eons. Each lesson has many levels of communication, deliberately installed. There are also three threads that run throughout all lessons. What you see within these lessons will depend on your perception, your astrological sign, your world view, your mind training, your shadows, your emotional training, your space within this stream cycle, and your philosophy. To some extent, this is a fact for everything and any event that comes in contact with you.

There are lessons between the lines, under the surface, waiting for you, and most certainly inside the exercises and meditations. As your meditation deepens and you experience your power and your personal core, you will be ushered into another frequency, so that you may see all that has been lovingly placed on these pages and in your life; that is, symbols, pictures, harmonic sounds, and colors that you have never experienced within this life. If this sounds impossible, I challenge you to do the exercises and see who you are by the end of these teachings. I challenge you to do the work and see the changes within you, changes that will reach the farthest four corners of earth, the four corners of the Universe.

Yet know that nothing has ever been hidden from you. You will receive the exact measure of what you put into this journey, no more and no less. If you do the work, you will increase your opportunity and ensure that your shadows and your promises will be revealed together, one diminishing while the other flows more fully through life.

Your true purposes may not be here, for only the changeable sea priestess will remain in these waters. This Path is *a* path, not *the* path, because everything is *the* path.

If you think becoming a Sea Priestess is focusing on things of the sea, you would be partly correct. It is essential, even paramount that we start with you and who you are. You will be untaught and asked to do much inner work to earn the title Sea Priestess. The title means nothing; claiming and changing your life are everything.

Here is the tough part: all outside gifts must be put down. The tarot, stones, herbs, charts, reference books, everything that has a perceived power must be stripped away, so that you may discover your own power, your own voice, and so that you may dig for your treasures, cultivating a direct line to all that is. Only after you have experienced and applied your treasures may you then pick up all those tools outside yourself to discover that they are more attuned to you, more powerful than before you laid them down. Stones, charts, herbs, and the tarot have incredible power, higher selves, and ever-expanding consciousness. As you install each helper back into your life, both you and your helpers will be more developed, strengthened to be able to hold the mantle of Sea Priestess, a living spring, directly connected to Source.

Untraining of a Sea Priestess

Sea Priestesses and Priests are "untrained"; by that I mean that we intentionally strip away previous trainings to uncover what lies beneath those layers. Then we are turned right-side out again, enabling us to uncover all our treasures and tools within. All people have been given so many untruths about their beings that have caused them not to live to their full potential. Once we identify those untruths that are holding us back, we are able to begin clearing that issue. Then we can continue to minister to the shadow places in our being, loving them by filling them with clear, pure, lighted water, a symbol of a real energetic process taking place.

When clearing is done, we can dig into ourselves to discover our tools and our heritage. Gifts surface to the top when the water becomes clear of those shadow places in our being; you begin to see through to the bottom of the cosmic ocean, and desire begins to encourage you to dig deeper.

Only then do we pick up our tools. It is one thing to dig for our tools, and it's quite another to pick up our tools and use them. An example: some of us enjoy the hunt, while others enjoy studying and thinking about the hunt someday. The hunt we study that never happens or the hunt that never ends are both beautiful in their own right, because these souls are working out lessons within themselves, which is always good.

Then we enter our divine purpose as a Sea Priestess, fully prepared to work as pioneers, doing our part. Yet remember, we were always inside our Divine purpose from the beginning; however, now we are conscious of and more aware of our Divineness and that our own Divineness can never be fully expressed apart from every being. Our Divineness can never be fully expressed through just this one life, yet we can gather everyone around and encourage everyone we are honored to meet.

Our sea heritage is the legacy of our ancestors traveling throughout the land and sea to find the others. United in these tasks, all Sea Priestesses and Priests come together.

We allow ourselves to end all outside stimuli, since everything outside us is robbing us of our time and our power. We focus instead on our work through these studies. We put down everything that hinders us from clearly seeing the big picture. By ending time-consuming outside influences, we may hear our own inner core, our own inner voice. Though books and other outside influences are good outside tools, but we cannot find out how we work, from where we came, and who we are from any single outside source. This untraining will push away all outside powers and push us into our power, our gifts, given directly to us. No middle man. Once again, books are good because they are signposts, helping us but nothing more.

Sea Priestesses are strong and have more stamina than any other energy. We know this inside. Sea Priests are fierce and have more gentleness than any other energy.

We know this inside. Both Sea Priestesses and Sea Priests have unending love. Like every being, we have no beginning nor end.

A Sea Priestess has a connection to water and water beings. The precepts of a Sea Priestess are called water mysteries, and a water being is any being affected by water, any being or place living inside, above, or beneath water—which, really, is *every* being. Every being has and is consciousness, thus everything lives and moves. Everything lives with water. Expanding this principle, the Universe is a water vessel that holds all consciousness.

When our focus is on fully being aware of our great gifts to the world, we realize that everyone is trying to learn how to actualize what we already hold within ourselves through water, which is full of unlimited possibilities. We instinctively know that we hold countless creations within us. We are learning how to bring these possibilities into existence. We are water beings, learning and experimenting with this wisdom, and so is everything else on this journey of reality awareness. Everything is showing everything else how they are learning actualization and forming reality.

Reading Is Not Enough

To know something is to experience it firsthand, not by receiving information secondhand or thirdhand, as this results in watered-down information. If you just read the words on these pages, not allowing the spirit behind the words to enter your life because you are not willing to fully experience and apply the pearl precepts within these lessons, then I hope you enjoy the words, as they will become seeds for the future. Reading mere words does not mean you know the precept; there are many hidden lessons that can be realized only when a Sea Priestess enters experiences fully, for only then will she be able to apply that knowledge. Only then is the precept genuinely her own. To truly understand these precepts, the Sea Priestess must not just read the words, but experience the lessons as well.

Through experience and concept application, there are so many more lessons to be revealed; they can be revealed only through action, through application, through full integration. Once you have entered into the experience, felt the experience firsthand, and applied the water of understanding to your life, only then are you an active participant. When you have done this, then you are not a spectator any longer but actively using your life as a force of nature, Sea Priestess!

Feel your very core energy. This is your time to develop and activate all your senses, all your gifts. You are interested in this subject because you have a deep, abiding sense of your purpose, but you also know that there are a few missing puzzle pieces to fulfill your calling. Or you may know your purpose and be ready to work for humanity. Or maybe you haven't discovered your purpose yet. By the end of these lessons, you will know, without a shadow of a doubt, of what you are capable, and you will be able to see everything with new eyes, through the lens of water.

As you travel across the seas through these lessons, you will see how shadows and water work together, unraveling your philosophy, unraveling you back to your very core. Generally, shadows are personality traits that cause an individual to be affected by fear, apathy, or pain, clouding most perceptions within one's life. A shadow is a part of us that has been shamed, or a part of us that is afraid, or a part of us that is insecure or has been hurt in the far past. These parts show up in many ways within our lives.

Water connects every living thing; water records all knowledge. Water lives inside all humans, animals, and plant life, and water seeks to clarify our perception. Water is consciousness and so are we. This strong tie helps humans see our shadows under water's sparkling light. Under the water's influence, we are ready to heal some of our shadows while diminishing others. From the first day, it is water that helped us learn, grow, and heal. Water is clarified as it heals our shadows. Water is also a spiritual platform on which all humans create their new life conditions. Water is a living consciousness, forever evolving. Our main focus throughout this book is you, because everything unfolds from there.

Perfection and spiritual maturity are already here through you.

☙ 1 ❧

Untangle

He who takes his teachings and applies them increases his knowledge.

—Hawaiian proverb

What Is on Your Head?

Many sponges, shells, and types of seaweed are used as protective coverings for inhabitants of the sea. They make a good hiding place for birthing young, a safe place to call a home, and provide a filter through which creatures can safely view their watery world. These are all good reasons to stay among the sanctuary of sponges and seaweed, but alas, young fish grow up and know, instinctively, it is time to come out of their protective coverings and to explore a wider world.

The same is true for a Sea Priestess. At a certain point, she will feel the urge to lay down all outside powers and external influences for a time and remove all shells that are now a burden. Just as the shells and seaweed protected young fish, these outside influences, too, have been helpful to the Sea Priestess but have now outgrown their purpose. Now is the time for you to come out of all the tangled seaweed that leads you to everywhere but you. The main purpose for this lesson is to gently untangle you from all overcomplications.

Over complication is a time and joy thief, designed to rob you of your free will, your Divine thoughts. Overcomplication gives you permission to struggle, because individuals have been trained that life and their "path" are one long, awful struggle. That is true only if you adopt that belief, thereby living under a shell that says that life is a struggle. If you have adopted this shell of struggle, it was a choice you made, likely long ago. It is not a good or bad choice, just a choice that needs to be reexamined.

Once you see the shell that you are wearing (be it of struggle or any other belief that you have held), you can decide if this choice is outdated or still useful for your growth; but only you can answer these questions. Be careful not to be swayed by what you may hear others say, as the truth that you are seeking can come only from inside yourself, not from external drama or stories.

As a Sea Priestess, you will see many different shells that you and those around you will wear to feel comfortable; yet know they, like you, are all just trying to find their way back home. Seeing problems from a new and different perspective allows us to begin our untraining and untangling from the seaweed in which we have become comfortable.

We have been taught that certain so-called truths will serve us well within our lives when, actually, they have been colossal blocks, veils, and strong sedatives that prevent us from living in our full potential. These so-called truths are designed to keep the waters of our mind and spirit muddy, so that we remain unmovable, unclear of our purpose, always trying to integrate with others instead of living through our own purpose. Through untraining, we discover the types of personalities around us from an objective stance and learn to navigate and clear the waters around us through our own power.

Personality Types and Veils

There are folks who desire to experience lessons through the veil (or shell) of need and/or some form of pain. There are others who enjoy the veil of drama. There are many other veils as well, and all are equally valid. No matter what veil or shell you are learning through, know that you selected this learning method for yourself and enjoy that choice. Some folks may enjoy wearing their veils. As unteachers, untanglers, and untrainers, you do not need to convince anyone to do anything. Remember that our main focus is on you, so as much as you may feel a need to convince others to do things differently, you are only a facilitator, helping unteach individuals that are of the sea; it is they that do the work, not you.

I believe that everyone inherently desires to be a true asset, genuinely desires to be the best person they can be. Some personalities are just trying to figure out how to show up in life; this does not make their veils good or bad, it is simply how they are interacting with the world. For example, let's say a person desires to become a leader. They believe that they were taught to put the spotlight on themselves, essentially saying, "Look at me." This person could undergo unteaching by instead putting the spotlight on the students and saying, "Look at you!" All their actions will convey that they are focused on the student, not the other way around, thus achieving their main goal of leadership without suffering or struggling—for them or the students.

Are you carrying an outgrown shell on your back? Ask yourself, "Why?" Are you lying immobile on a sea sponge, doing nothing? Ask yourself, "Why?" Are you tangled among the high seaweed, causing you to not see the Universe's vistas? There is a reason, but you must ask.

Today, before you read one more word, identify what is holding you back from what you want in your life. Ask yourself, "What are my shadows?" You do know what they are. Lay down everything you perceive as a sponge, outgrown shell, or seaweed shadow field. Let us pretend that we are given only one life—ask yourself, "Am I living life to the fullest? Am I helping others? Am I relying on others to tell me what my shadows are? Am I relying on outside things to tell me about myself?"

If the questions are difficult to answer, do not worry; that is why you are here. Through this work, you will begin to clear the waters, to make a path, and to become a Sea Priestess, receiving instruction from the best teacher on earth—you!

Our Shadows

Although we think we see the world clearly, we actually see through a veil, or many veils. We think we know what reality is for ourselves and even for others, but we do not. Some veils have been lovingly placed on us by our parents, by our teachers, by our friends, by our culture, but most are by our own hand. We think we have keen insight on other people's lives, interpreted not as they really are but seen through veils on our own head. Some of us think our training and experience are superior to any other training or culture. We value or devalue others by our own shadow's impossible standards, which only causes us to move apart from one another, instead of moving closer.

But we can change this. We only need to focus on dissolving our shadows while other individuals focus on dissolving their own shadows, bringing everyone back into the World Ocean, where we are all supporting and affecting one another, even as we cultivate our own water energy field. We are rewarded when we work on our shadows. As we explore our shadows, our gifts automatically rise up to replace every shadow that is dissolved. Situations change around us, because we change. As we change, we may find it easier to lay down our attention on the physical realm and replace it with Spirit, but we must never lose focus on the practicality of these lessons, for it is important to have one foot in both worlds.

Exploration beyond the physical brings all of us to a place where our focused thoughts become our reality, where we realize that all realities are mutable. All physical realities are a veil. To enter the portal of cosmic omnipresence is to look beyond our physicality, beyond our mentality, to run toward the limits of reality and to find none! Thus boundaries are eliminated. As Westerners, we are too focused on the body and the ego-conscious mind, thus our perceptions are very tied to those very small aspects, instead of the larger, nonlinear systems.

We are all here learning and experiencing different lessons that we pre-chose before we popped into this reality plane. We chose to be here and to hopefully experience life to its fullest. Yet some people go out of their way to do the opposite, to keep from fully living. Due to our choices, we all perceive our world as reality and, truthfully, it is not reality in its fullness; it is only a small part of the entire picture. Our limited minds cannot perceive all of what is right here, right now; however, our Divine

Mind, our mind that is connected to all and is created out of wholeness, can and is connected to all realities.

Open-minded folks excel at this concept. These are people who are willing to step out of their minds/shells to enter their Divine Mind through meditation, deep lucid dreaming, astral journeying, and/or living life in full. It is important to understand that people work on different life lessons, using different methods. No two people have the same reality or the same consciousness; however, we all are able to clearly see and explore our Divine connection through us, not through anyone apart from us.

Some Realities by Which Good Individuals Live

Throughout the decades, I have heard many different stories from those around me. People say: "I have no control of what happens to me" or "I have created my life by my own hands"; "Success comes easily" or "Success is difficult to achieve"; "Life is peace" or "Life is a constant struggle." You get the picture.

Every one of those quotes is true in this reality system. None of these stories are bad or good, they are only present experiences and lessons to be learned. No one is wrong. Each person is seeing their reality through their own shadows, their own veils, through their own eyes. Each person pulls that veiled reality into their lives, which leads them to think everyone lives their way. They do not. Not everyone approaches life the same way, which is a good thing. Life would be incredibly boring if we were all learning the same lessons in the same way.

There are times when we need to take a closer look at what we are learning and ask if it is time to move on to our next lesson. Moving on is identifying and removing distortions and filters that we think are protecting us when, in fact, they are not.

Be gentle with yourself when you ask the following questions to judge whether it is time for you to move on and begin to remove your veils and filters. Ask yourself if you are capable of living life to the fullest. It is sad to say that some folks say "no," and we wish them all the best. Ask yourself the hard questions surrounding your veils. Examine all your excuses, but know that there are no real reasons to hold yourself back. A person may have one or two excuses, and they, indeed, can be valid; however, if a person shoots excuses out like a machine gun, then they are not ready to move forward. This person needs to ask the dreaded question, "Why?"

The mind (with a small "m"), or the base mind, has a zillion whys; ultimately, all these individual's excuses will make it difficult for them to remove their veils. What restrictions are you placing on yourself? Whom are you blaming? Are you allowing your past or your fears to make your decisions for you? There is not one excuse we can use that can stop us, even if the excuse is "I have nothing!" That is still not a valid reason not to move forward and to achieve what you desire. You have everything you need inside you; you just do not fully know it yet. I speak out of experience when I say, "Out of nothing, I created something."

It frightens some people to think that we are directly connected to everything, thus it scares us to take on accountability and find answers for ourselves. Once again, because we are so physically oriented, time- and space-bound, all these boundaries become our veils, making us forget what we have learned in past lives and causing apathy in our current lives! Thus fear becomes a security blanket that we hold on to for dear life.

All of us know deep within our souls that we are working on a much larger plan than any human behavior modality has ever fathomed. We are getting glimpses of how big we are. All our varied aspects of our developments are, in fact, Divinity's development through us. Divinity cannot be complete without us. Divinity cannot grow apart from us. We are her hands, we are her eyes, we are her voice, we are her movement. She explores herself through us. She unfolds herself through us. She expands through us as we expand through her.

> *Since everything is but an apparition, perfect in being what it is, having nothing to do with good or bad, acceptance or rejection, one may well burst out in laughter.*
> —Tibetan Buddhist teacher, Longchenpa

Then We Die

It is the ego-centered mind that runs amok, reminding us, ultimately, that there is death and there is an end, which is the biggest cosmic lie of all. The ego says we will "die," but the Universe says, "How can consciousness die?" It can't, thus we can't; it is an impossibility.

Some people use death as a veiled threat to hang over our head, but death is just a veil/shell. Some may use the possibility of death as a roadblock to keep from living fully, cluttering minds with falsehoods and hopelessness. Many have been taught that "death" is what happens at the end of our lives. When we begin to deal with death, we are then enabled to live—really live! Some say we die; I say that's not true. How can we fear death when our being, who we really are, does not die but is always in a transitional state. Fear is one of the main joy thieves that cause us to become unfocused or negative; the very opposite of what we have been designed to express. Fear of death causes us to go into a kind of sleep and stay there until we so-called "die."

Death shall never touch us, my beauties, never. It is an impossibility. Death cannot destroy us nor cause us to disappear or be diminished in any way, for even our physical bodies become food for Mother Earth. Death is a life gate that we enter both ways. We enter the other side, and we enter this side—never exiting, only entering. Death is only an illusion of many illusions. We are Spirit, wearing a wonderful earth suit made of skin, blood, and bone.

We are not our skin, we are not our blood, and we are not our bones. We are only borrowing this body so that we may move through this life on this side of the life gate. We are too hung up on this earth suit, relating everything to it. Yes, we should respect and take care of our bodies, because our bodies for most of us are serving us well, but they are not us.

We are much more than this illusion. We have always been, we are always now, and will always be Goddess/God/Source. We have always been the Sea Priestesses of the Goddess. We were here in the beginning, and we are here at the end, within this reality system. Outside this physical system, there is no beginning or end; we have always been and will always be. Never diminishing, ever expanding, and ever growing brighter.

No one can kill us, nothing can make us die, because Spirit, energy, or Deity cannot be killed. We are pure light energy, made of the same stuff as the most distant stars and seas. We are made of Divine substance, connected to and part of Deity, complete in this very moment. Only the physical body experiences death, or does it? The body only changes to another beautiful frequency. We are much larger than our earth suits. So-called "death" is only replacing our earth suits as we enter another frequency.

We do not die. We can't. We continue to live in our fullness, we continue to live in our completeness, we continue to live within our Divinity, our consciousness and Divine consciousness remain forever.

To live on this side of the life gate is to be completely connected to Source, to live in the Divine now with all its marvels of what is. To live on the other side is to be completely connected to Source, to live in the Divine now with all its marvels of what is. On both sides, we live in the Divine now. When we are on this side, we are learning to see everything in this now, within this moment, to see what is pure illusion and what is not. We are not here to be controlled by fear; we are here to be and experience what we really are: Divine and completely connected to a loving Deity. In a cosmic sense, there is no there, just here. Everything on earth proclaims, "We reside within her." We are masters of our own life because it is our life.

If we want to change what we are receiving in life, we must change how we feel about life. We must begin to see others for who they really are: Divinity. We must allow all garbage/veils/shells to die, allow all hurt to die, allow all fear, all resentment, and all hate to die. Allow the water to become clear. If we want things to change outside us, we must first change our own perspective by working through our own shadows. Instead of allowing veils to diminish us, we must diminish them. When we clear our waters, fear loses its control over us and instantly dissolves into nothing. We are here to learn how to wake up and to experience the Divine on this side of the life gate.

When it is time to enter the other side, guess what? We are there to learn and experience the Divine also, and to see things much more clearly than we can from this side. We are forever. You are forever.

Untangling Resources

Meditation #1

With your eyes closed, ground by diving into the deepest sea. Release your thoughts by allowing the ocean to move through you. Invoke the Fostering Mother of the Sea to show herself to us this moment. Invoke your guides to prepare your ears to hear. Relax and allow the sea essence to enter your being like water entering the ocean from a white waterfall above. Feel her love engulf you completely.

You will hear the Goddess speak as if she lives inside you. She invites you to remove all distortions, veils, shells, and filters that you believe are protecting you; they are not. She reminds you that you have control of your life, and you have everything you need to live the life you have chosen.

She shows you that while most experiences are seen as external events, they are not; instead, external events are the projections of our life lessons and our perceptions, reflecting the reality that we have created internally. She encourages you to discover the truth that there is no loss, only change—from life to life, breathing and not breathing and breathing again—because you are an interdimensional being, a living ceremony, a spiritual energy field working within a larger water energy field. She reveals that perfection and spiritual maturity are already here living through you.

Common Questions for a Sea Priestess

Many Sea Priestesses have come to me with the following questions and comments. Because they are common concerns, I would like to share them with you so that, if they resonate with you, you can benefit from their thoughts. I have included this section in each chapter to help you to dive deeper into your Sea Priestess practice.

I have so many shadows.

> One answer that I give to Sea Priestesses with this problem is to ask them: "Are you sure they are all your shadows?" Look at each shadow; are they really shadows? Approach your problems by being solution oriented. Focus on the solution, not the problem.

What if I am already perfectly content with my life?

> My suggestion then is to simply enjoy it! Continue helping this earth and its people flourish! Once we fully understand ourselves, then it is time to turn outward and help our hurting Mother Earth and all she loves.

If there's no such thing as death, what do you call it when we are put in a coffin, six feet under the ground? Isn't that death?

> This question can be difficult to deal with, but I ask you to understand that the body is not us. Even that body is not disappearing, it is changing into another form; yet at its core, like the most distant star, it has all the sameness as anything else. Our consciousness decides to transition into another reality system or come back into this reality. There is no end, no "death"—only change.

Why is the discussion of death important?

Death is one of the great universal fears shared by most individuals. If we look death squarely in the face, we begin to see it for what it isn't. Fear of death loses its grip on us, thus allowing us to dive deeper into our purpose and this life. If we dissolve this fear, then we can deal with all the other shadows and see them for what they really are: thieves of our joy and of our lives! We, in turn, will stop giving our fears power and render *them* useless, not us.

Exercise #1

Identifying Excuses

Use the prompt below to create a list of free-association excuses by listing the first twenty-five words or phrases that come to mind in response to the prompt.

My excuses for not attaining what I want are:

_____

Once you have your rapid-fire answers, look at those words and feel the emotion from every one of them: the fear, the insecurity, etc. Look at them and see them for what they are really doing to you: they are controlling you. Recall that your excuses are produced by your shadows; so what shadows do you need to change to attain what you want? All shadow indicators can be changed, each one of them! If you *think* you have the power to change or dismiss your shadow indicators, you do; if you think you cannot, then you cannot. Nothing can stand between your goal and you. Nothing!

Exercise #2

What Do You Look Like?

Draw or paint what you think you look like, as a Divine, Spirit, energy being. Ask your Higher Self for help. Relax; make this assignment an exploration of Self. Allow this assignment to touch your soul!

Allow yourself to see through the waters. Allow your veil to be blown away by the trade winds of change. Only you can remove your outworn perceptions. Remove the veil to reveal your crown!

What is that on your head? A crown!

∽ 2 ∾

Release: There Goes a Frog

Since once I sat upon a promontory, and heard a Mermaid on a dolphin's back uttering such dulcet and harmonious breath, that the rude sea grew civil at her song and certain stars shot madly from their spheres, to hear the sea-maid's music.
—William Shakespeare, A *Midsummer Night's Dream*

In this lesson, we shall continue to work on our transformation into a Sea Priestess by focusing on releasing our outer tools, so that we may activate our inner treasures. A Sea Priestess possesses all her tools within; she needs no tools outside herself. The Universe has equipped us completely, without anything lacking. We are the altar, we are the moon, we are the sea, we are the manifestation mechanism. We work with archetypes, or work with none; we are the stars, we are the waters, both within this physical land and in deep space. We are one being experiencing everything here. We are transitioners working with the powerful tool called love while healing our shadows as each day goes by.

Let us begin to remove everything outside us so that we are able to see all our frogs. Frogs are when the Universe speaks to us through an animal or any living symbol. The frog represents anything in nature that crosses your path and teaches you something regarding your life. It does not need to be a frog specifically; it can be a leaf or gentle wind blowing across your face that is communicating with you. The "frog" desires to help you see your reality more clearly.

When symbols (frogs) come to us, we often go speeding to a symbol dictionary or a dream encyclopedia or any number of outside references to help us determine the meaning of the symbol we have found. There is nothing wrong with having a fun conversation about what our frogs mean or in using written information to back up our beliefs, but we must not forget to consult the frog itself, instead of disconnecting from the message it is conveying. It is easier to look up what frog means than to commune with frog and find out for ourselves. By connecting to nature firsthand, we connect to our true nature and intelligence.

For this reason, I suggest starting your own frog journal, where you can keep track of the frogs that you have found and what meanings they have conveyed to you. Your journal will reveal that you do not need anything outside yourself; that you, indeed, are perfectly equipped to interpret your frog yourself. All associations need to be meaningful to you and your life, not simply what someone outside yourself has said.

Depending on your culture, age, tradition, gender, or world view, it can be incredibly important to ask Spirit what any water association means, including the frog. It is fun to find out how the ancient people would assign different properties to different elements; however, it is imperative we find out what properties a "creature" has that directly relate to our life. Direct information from nature and spirit is best. I often hear people say, "Yes, however it is easier to just go to a book." It is, and this may possibly be a good starting point; but also consider: what kind of genuine connection can you foster if you are simply reading someone else's interpretation of your direct message from a frog spirit? Each shell, stone, or frog desires to work directly with us.

As Sea Priestesses, we must be willing to lay down reference books for a while so that we may pick up our own interpretation tools—when we are working with all nature, but especially with water and water creatures. We do have an interpretation tool inside us called "discernment."

Laying down all outside tools allows us to remember how we have laid down our own power in the past. It is now time to regain that which we so freely gave up. Some of us are so quick to turn our power over to something or someone outside ourselves, we then wonder why we cannot gain anything substantial, saying to ourselves, "No matter what path I walk, I will never experience fulfillment." Sea priestesses' untraining reveals this statement as an untruth. All we lovingly desire is incredibly reachable.

How we retain or give our power away by choosing what to believe is the way that we walk through life. For some, it is natural to go to the negative side instead of the positive side of most situations. Some have been trained to interpret most issues in a negative manner. Untraining says that we must first look at what we are, what tools we possess, and what we know; we must stop looking for answers outside our Divine Self. Sea Priestesses are first and foremost independent thinkers and agents of change. We are the natural portal to our full life; nothing outside us holds our free will. Every being is a natural portal to a full life, but this truth has been kept hidden from the masses. The masses are beginning to see this truth once again and regain their full authority within their own lives, which touches everyone's lives within and without their sphere of influence.

Some see the light in a flash; these folks have already done much of their work in past lives. Some see the light with lots of small "aha" moments. Some "see" the light as a lotus flower, slowly opening, slowly unfolding before their eyes, slowly sinking below the water's surface at night, then rising above the water's surface to see the light under the morning sun.

By laying down all outside sources of so-called power, we create new brain neuron pathways within our watery brains, so that we may reconstruct old thinking patterns that have not served us well in the past. By identifying how we think or how we have been taught to think, we begin to understand that it is easier to focus on the negative than to focus on manifestation-producing positive frequencies. Consistent negative thoughts are nothing but blocks to what we desire. Positive emotions have been kicked out of us throughout our lives, and the keys to our treasure chests were ripped from our holy hands.

The Sea Priestess's key to open the treasure chest, the fountain of knowledge, has been here all along; however, all our shadow symptoms have blinded us to it. As we remove or love each shadow, the key becomes clearer within our own hands, because the shadows begin to clear. The key has always been in our hands and a part of us. The key opens our treasure chest. It is rightfully ours as Sea Priestesses. Our treasure chest is where all our tools are for safekeeping, and when we are fully aware of our radiant light and ready to reclaim our life, it can be opened by us only through purposeful joy.

Now is the time to open this chest, to relearn all our magical water tools. As we relearn, we become a treasure to this planet; we are gifts to the world.

Belief Systems

Belief systems behave just like frogs; it is belief that gives meaning to our lives. Our shadows produce symptoms or conditions that allow us to be pushed around and trained to accept belief systems that keep us from seeing our own capabilities. Shadows, in and of themselves, need our attention to be loved away and healed by water's highest frequency. A very close friend of mine takes care of her shadows by giving them love and attention, informing them that they will be healed and be transformed into something good once more. Some individuals make all their decisions and form every belief system based on fear, while others stop living a full life and form belief systems based on shame. This is why it is so imperative to deal with broken belief systems and begin focusing on letting go to move forward.

Our belief systems are the base of all our strong core feelings, which in turn generate vibrations. These strong feelings cause vibrations to be sent out into the universal oceans to be created! Good, bad, or indifferent, our beliefs come back to us like a boomerang. This is why they say, "Be careful what you wish for, because you may receive it." Whatever we send out on a consistent basis with strong emotion is what the Universe receives and sends back, created by none other than us.

No belief system is better than another belief system. We only need to discover which belief systems are hindering us and which systems are propelling us closer to our fullness. It is imperative to discover how we tick, and how we either block or set things in motion within our life. You can do this by gently becoming aware of yourself, by paying attention to your continual thought patterns, thus identifying your belief systems. Then ask each belief system, "Are you presently serving me well?" You must then allow your life to answer the question.

A belief system begets strong feeling, begets strong vibration, begets our life. This is why it is important to discover our core beliefs. Strong emotions live within all belief systems. Beliefs around money are good examples of belief systems that hold strong emotions for many individuals.

As an example, answer the following questions regarding money to see what your belief systems around it are:

- What do you think about money?
- What do you think about rich individuals?
- What do you think about individuals who have little money?
- Are you satisfied with the amount of money you now have? Why?
- Is it difficult to gain money? If yes, why?
- Is it difficult to save money? If yes, why?

I selected this belief system as an example to show how we react to our beliefs; in this example, to money. This is one belief system that causes emotions to rise in many individuals. We create our own belief system, then our belief system forms our life. The best way to counteract the unconscious acts is to begin to identify our belief systems day by day, focusing on one at a time, generally. If you are thinking, "I cannot change how I think," you are right. You've just discovered another belief system—that you will never change how you think—and because you believe it, it is true for you.

Sea Magic, the magic of a Sea Priestess, is about continual transformation. Some changes will take decades; some changes take months; others will take place in a twinkling of an eye, in a split second, in a snap; while still other changes may take lifetimes to be realized. Isn't magic about transformation? For a Sea Priestess, it certainly is. Our beliefs mold us; that is why we need to identify our beliefs—so that we may mold them.

The point of a Sea Priestess's untraining is to find where we are controlled by what we think and to change that belief so that we control what we are by what we decide to deliberately feel. Our mind does not control us; it is we who control our magical mind. Our mind does not tell us what to do or think; it is we who inform our mind what to do or think, thus forming new realities through new belief systems.

Let us say you desire to live an abundant life. But you have a strong mistrust of those who have an abundant life, however you define abundance. This is a belief system that will not allow your desire for abundance to come to pass. By removing this distrustful belief system, you remove a self-made block designed by one of your shadows. Your shadows should not be running your life; it is you that is running your life.

Like most metaphysical truths, this process sounds easy except for all the training we have had to chronically sell ourselves short. It takes courage to call forth all tools that are rightfully ours to create our lives from this day forward. It takes a strong, courageous woman or man to love our shadows back to light.

Our regeneration begins now! We have been told all our life, in so many ways, so very often, that we are not enough. The answers are someplace "out there in the distance," never near or in us. However, we are more than enough; we all have the capacity to change this world.

Now we shall begin to break down the walls, kicking out any teaching that has caused disconnection between us and our own life. We have been told it is natural to swim upstream, that life is always a struggle. We have been told that we need this thing outside us to look better, to be validated, to have fun—we need, need, need. We were taught that as a belief system, so that we could become a good little consumer or stay inside the lines, become a conformist. Heaven forbid, do not rock the boat!

Many belief systems have been installed to keep us feeling we are in lack, always wanting. Because of this, we are incessantly wanting, taught to be never satisfied, causing a huge disconnection from our own full creature-hood. How does that make us feel? Yes, there are several legitimate reasons why we have not received what we thought we deserved or even needed. Yes, there are karmic issues, unresolved hidden issues, and the ever-present disconnection that must be addressed; however, all are based on old belief systems—every one of them.

Conversely, none of these issues are outside our reach to change. Let us pretend we have no blocks at all. None. Let us pretend that our creator made us into what she is: a wise, strong creator.

Let us imagine we were not told, "You cannot do that," "You cannot experience that," "You cannot have that," "You cannot be that." Now let us imagine that we do not believe what "they" have said. Let us imagine reality is not what we were told it is, that it is an ever-fluid, ever-changing stream created by us. Let us imagine that we do not have a deep-seated belief system that tells us we do not deserve a big wonderful life. Let us pretend we were told all our life that we can lead a beautiful life! Let us imagine we made a sound decision to change our life today, because we believe we can reach our goals; it is our life and we get to decide on how we live it in graceful empowerment.

What do we think would happen if we changed our mind-set, changing what we expect from ourselves and our lives? We just changed a belief system, thus changing us, and all we imagined became reality, our reality. No one is saying this is easy—both ways of thinking have ramifications—and living deliberately is not easy either, yet overcoming our limiting beliefs is a prize indeed.

Releasing Resources

Meditation #1

The entire Universe is slowly unfolding before us! See our promise. The Sea Priestess enters, saying nothing is needed, for we have already been given everything we need, gifts from the sea. Guide my thoughts and every deed, that I may fulfill our prophecy.

Common Questions for a Sea Priestess

I have so many problems. I need to talk about my problems.

It is good to talk about problems for a little while. Not for five years. It is good to talk about problems only if we desire to come out of our problems and stay focused on solutions and moving forward. By keeping our focus on action-oriented solutions, problems begin to dissolve in time.

What if I am not interested in living an abundant life?

Perfect, your life is yours to mold any way you like. However, abundance is defined by you. Abundance is different for everyone; there is no one definition of what it should be.

Exercise

What Do You Want?

This may sound like an easy question, but try the exercise below:

Set a timer for fifteen minutes. In that time period, write down twenty-five of your wishes. To dig deeper, try doing it for thirty minutes.

For most of us, this assignment is startlingly difficult. We have given up wishing, as if wishing were a negative or were somehow untrue. It is as if we do not dare wish for something good for us! One of our purposes is to create our world. Wishing is part of the key to creating what we want and need. If the word "wishes" bothers you, then replace it with "prayers," "requests," or "dreams."

Next, set the timer for fifteen minutes again; this time write down twenty-five negative things about your life.

This is going to be much easier for some because our reality/mundane world is defined by negatives. In fact, some of us define ourselves in negative terms. Example: I don't believe in that religion, or I do not believe I can do it. But defining who you are *not* is not the same as defining who you *are*. Plus, it only sends negative vibrations, which do not help anyone, including you. Now evaluate your list. You have just identified many of your belief systems.

Focus on the feeling of each "wish item" and each negative item on your lists. Which wishes bring up the most feelings within you? Which negative items make you feel the most strongly? You have now found the pressure points that cause you to pull your wishes into your life. The pressure points of what you desire will come into your physical world. You see part of what you are by what you want.

3

Dreaming

The sage's transformation of the world arises from solving the problem of water.

—Lao Tzu

Many of us, as humans, have been painstakingly trained to dream small, so if our dreams are crushed, it will not harm us as much. This upside-down thinking has rendered some humans completely helpless and powerless. It is this thinking that seemingly unplugs us from our infinite Higher Self, our expanded self, and blurs our connection to our loving Source that created us from the very beginning.

To look at ourselves with new eyes is scary for some, yet it is important to learn and to utilize all our senses to receive all that is rightfully ours. Our five senses have been dulled to the point that we do not clearly see what is right in front of us or hear what is being communicated now by another human, let alone one of our guides or our Higher Self.

Through the centuries, many of our physical senses have been trained out of us while other senses have been completely hidden. We have been trained to believe untruths about our own being and trained that it is crazy to think that we have more senses than our five dull physical senses. We are more than what we have been taught. We are much more.

This is why it is important to begin exercising all our physical senses in new ways. This is why it is so important to exercise our chakras, because there are myriad senses and personifications that are buried deep under false training. As Sea Priestesses, we strip away anything that dulls our senses and keeps us weighed down. Let us begin to consider that all our senses are bigger and more refined than we ever imagined before; begin to imagine that all the senses we possess are more relevant than we ever imagined.

To expand your senses, send your intention out toward the sea by saying, "I desire to open my eyes to see what I shall see." Focus on one sense at a time for one month, or as long as you need to open your senses. Remember that there are many ways to see; one does not need eyes to see or a tongue to communicate. Then you will whisper the following incantation, without flinching.

It does not matter if you believe what you say in the mantra, just consider each word as a seed that will grow until you do. Take deep breaths as you proclaim what you are.

I was wonderfully made by the light.

I was created by a love so deep and vast, that she made me complete from the beginning. I am the embodiment of she who made me. I am part of Deity Consciousness.

I am remembering who I am. I chose to be here, this way, in this time.

I am all that is needed to express the infinite all that is.

I am magnificent.

I am magical.

I am more than enough.

I am loved beyond measure, beyond time, beyond space.

I have everything I need within to live my life.

The Universe cannot complete this big beautiful experiment without me! I am needed, all my talents are needed to make this world heal, and it cannot without me!

My own body is a healer.

I created many places before I decided to come here within this reality, to help others home. My Source moves through me; I *am* Source, through and through. I am fully capable of finding and utilizing all my gifts.

I am not less, I am more.

After reading these truths aloud, check in with your body. Are you still breathing? What are you feeling? Did you feel walls being built up or being torn down as you proclaimed these truths? Did you feel undeserving, not worthy of such love and attention? Now let us identify all the concepts that have caused us to be unreactive in this world and the worlds around and within us.

The second we plug into our expanded self/Higher Self, as a champion and hero, is the second we begin to see "where" we think and that our mind is bigger than what fits within our skull. We begin to utilize all of our guidance systems and meet all those who have been with us, waiting for us to get our show on the road by living life! Everything and every life story starts with a single consistent thought. Unfocused, scattered thoughts are counted and cause our dreams, our wishes, to become scattered and unfocused.

Throughout the ages, power-hungry control freaks have kept that a secret from the brilliant masses, because they were under the false notion that only a few royals, a few cleric leaders, and some government officials needed to know such a great truth—that our minds control our reality. They thought the masses were below them and needed to be controlled. These belief systems caused many wars throughout history and continue to do so.

Mankind, based on this false belief system, set up thousands of other belief systems, formal and informal, all designed to control the brilliant masses. As centuries passed, the walls were built high and thick around most cultures, so by the time Universal truths surfaced again, as they always do, the brilliant masses were trained to not see what they were; some peoples had even become completely disconnected from themselves and from the gateway to their Source and championship. The arrogant discredited anyone who would dare to live in any other way than what they had taught the brilliant masses to believe.

The arrogant people were under the false impression that if everyone led a brilliant life, it would somehow diminish their own lives and make them lesser. This greed for power and control has started every war on this earth. The untraining is the concept that there is no such thing as a pie in the sky that needs to be divided among everyone. There is enough for everyone, leaving no one lacking. Disrespecting our Sources causes lack. Never sharing, never seeding, never harvesting causes lack; not giving everyone every opportunity causes lack.

Let us unplug from the noise of the world that does not support us as humans and plug into seriously focusing on what is possible.

It is impossible to ever be cut off from our Self and our Source. We have been trained not to see what we are and what we are fully capable of doing and giving. Now is the time when the truth is handed to the brilliant masses on a silver platter. Some of the brilliant masses will say, "How? I can't understand! It can't be true" and walk away. Some individuals have been trained to be fearful of new ways; they are troubled or even wrong. They say, "For years, we have set up societies this way, so it must be right!"

Do not judge this type of person. We will slowly love them into knowing and away from the low-vibration, collective social consciousness. One does not need to explain this great truth to them; we only need to love them, and they will come to discover it for themselves.

The light is too bright for the negative base consciousness, or an ego-centered mind, to fully understand, let alone apply, these truths. It is impossible for them to do so—by choice. They stop themselves from understanding as Goddess patiently waits for them. "Groups" have formed through the ages to study these strange truths and purposely made them stranger to keep them hidden from the brilliant masses. Books have been written, religions formed, meetings held—all trying to understand with the ego-centered mind. Base thinkers try to understand mere words through low-vibrational, base social consciousness, not seeing their own Higher Self.

But now we are ready and able to be untrained back to the light. These are some reasons why we need to make the switch, to think with all our minds, and receive untwisted information with our entire, fully capable beings. Following directions from our Higher Self and getting connected to our guidance system never lead us astray. This is doable for everyone.

From a young age, we were taught to second-guess our feelings, our reasoning, to the point that some individuals wait to find out what others are thinking before deciding what to think about their own life. I do not know of anything sadder than not trusting your own person, your own self. Meeting our guides, all our helpers, causes us to be connected to our unseen minds and potential. All the answers to all our questions are within us. There is nothing outside us.

Maybe for the first time in your life, you have begun to discover how many ways you receive information and how many new ways you can feel your way back home. No one is able to think themselves back home. Every molecule has a consciousness; all atoms within you are waiting to be expressed, even teach. Every blade of grass and every mountain is part of you, too, waiting to be utilized by you. We select other people's belief systems and "think" they are ours, but they are not. We believe the incessant chatter of the ego-centered mind and base social consciousness, but neither are hard-wired to our Higher Self. This means that while we are in them, we are completely capable of untraining and forming our own belief systems and becoming more aware of our own reality systems.

As we move forward, we need to be willing to look at our own divinity, our Higher Selves, with brand new Sea Priestess eyes. With these eyes, you will look at each tool as a golden key that not only opens you but also opens many worlds. These tools are keys to changing us back to what we were, all the while evolving forward, if we are willing to walk into our fullness as what we were originally made to be: loving heroes and artists. Every step we take, every key we select, will result in our abundance, our expansion.

First, get connected to your own Higher Self, then go! Do! Learn about what you feel, not what someone else says you should feel; what you see, what you reveal. It is we who select what we believe, no one else. We cannot blame anyone else. We are the ones who insert the key into the lock, turn the key, then turn the knob to enter into the life we want to live. Only we walk through the door we have opened. Not our boss, not our family, not our spiritual leaders; nobody can unlock our wonders but us.

Just by identifying the little complaining, judgmental, insecure, low-vibration thinker inside us is a huge step and will cause many "aha!" moments. Deity is waiting for us to come into our fullness, to the eternal temple that we formed before we wore skin. We will also see how only one key (or tool) can open more than one door for us. All keys and tools intersect one another, so do not be surprised when you get an "aha!" moment and other fuzzy concepts become crystal clear in a second.

Flip the Switch

We are created to create, by deciding (wishing/dreaming) what we want, then calling it forth in countless ways. We are to enjoy the journey as we move through this life.

It is not wrong to desire; it is natural. That is what creators do! They create out of their desires. How do you think the wheel was invented? Someone wanted to move something forward; out of that want came the stone wheel, which eventually benefitted everyone on this planet. Someone wanted to move faster, so a wooden wheel was invented that benefitted the entire world once again, and so on, and so on.

Our deepest desires are where our glory and gifts are located and unleashed on this world, through us, to the benefit of all. If we receive what makes us happy, everyone benefits! We do not need to go to a dark place to work on our shadows, though "dark" does not mean "bad." Light and dark have no judgment. There are no shadows in the dark, only in the light.

There are three main shadows: shame, fear, and insecurity. Every thought, action, or reaction comes from either shadow or love. We do not need to know about or "get to the root" of every shadow we have. If we analyze our shadows, then we are utilizing the ego-centered mind.

To get in touch with your shadows and to convey love to them, say the following affirmation:

> I open my mind's eye so that I may deeply see my heritage, through second sight.
>
> I release the intoxicating fragrance of my love and my light. I remove the many shadows that others have placed over my sight. I remove the many shadows that I have placed over my own sight.
>
> I allow my sea song to well up, like the living waters from where I came. Like a true Sea Priestess, I will light my shadows with a loving fire, burning away

all outgrown precepts, and love my shadows in the ocean's flame.

I allow my heart to hear my true sacred voice, my guides' voices, my Goddess, my God. I open every thought and overfill my cup with your wisdom, your promises, your thoughts, my wisdom, my promises, my thoughts.

I will receive through strong waves of emotional delight all that I am. In every way, every day, always following your song, which is my song.

I will move with the tides and the springs within. I will have the courage to rest within myself, my Deity. In the deep waters I remain.

Reasons

We receive in many ways and we interpret everything, every day, through all our veiled senses. To see more clearly or to become more aware of what and how we receive, we only need to purposefully open our hearts to Divinity and to ourselves. Removing our self-imposed limits allows us to see Deity within ourselves and every living creature and non-creature.

As we continue to "Know Thyself," we see and feel our internal guidance system in pure love, given freely by the Goddess. Divine love is not a friend's love, a pet's love, a significant other's love. Nor is Divine love self-love, a mother's love, a father's love.

Divine love is experiencing being. This world already is Divine love; it's only the human race that needs to stop harming each other, stop shedding blood. When the human race loves itself, it will see it is Divine love ushering in a host of discoveries that will sustain nonviolence. Divine love includes all the kinds of love listed above plus much more. When we stop actively harming the human race as well as all the other natural kingdoms, we will then fully accept how Divine we are.

Goddess is love. God is love. It would take one million libraries to define Divine love. Only after we stop harming ourselves will we begin to understand human love and Divine love.

We see our world more clearly when our motives are based on love; everything builds upon the other, each life concept is a life changer within itself, yet all creatures are different and seemingly independent of one another. Because we do not love ourselves, we reason our desires away. Not making room for the desires in our lives causes us to become undone. We are hopeful in very short spurts, because we come up with dozens of reasons why we are not receiving what we have asked for. Some of us reason our wishes away.

Reasoning can only focus on "what is happening now" and cannot fathom beyond already manifested reality; it cannot understand untraining. When desires are reasoned away, we are not wide-open receptors, we are not paintbrushes or strings being played. Remember that we hold the paintbrush in our hands, and it is we who play the music. There is information coming in and information going out. The information going out should be focused on actions taken now. Information is not completely understood until it is used.

When we see how many ways we receive information, from many different sources, we begin to directly plug into our holy Source. In other words, from source to Source, from Source to source. We see how much control we have over our lives. We realize our beautiful Universe has never stopped speaking to us from the beginning, showing us that all along we have been communicating with Deity. Deity has always carried us and always will; even the wind rejoices with us. We all have been taught the slick reasons why not to live in fullness. Each excuse or reason is a self-imposed veil.

But what we say to ourselves does not matter. All that matters is how we communicate our desires to the Universe. Communicating our desires through strong, open, joy-filled emotion lines us up with the same high frequency that makes desires become reality. Living in pure joy opens everything, even in tragedy. Living in bliss does not mean we will not experience hardship in our lives, it just means we know we are love. To know how we receive and feel is to know how we send our desires out to be manifested.

We open our receivers through the high-frequency vibration of pure joy and love. If we are too busy focusing on what we already have, we only get more of the same. For many of us, joy and love are tremendously difficult to enter and express, because all feelings have been kicked out of us. But our joy was a key to crank our vibrations up, way up, to a higher frequency, where all the action is located.

The Universe is only delivering what we are sending—nothing more, nothing less. No one can do this for us; it is we who turn up the volume.

Through joy and love we find our way, our love, and our song from the sea's heart. Love and joy are the motive for our journey, the beginning of the process, what we were, and what we are. We do not need to worry about how our desires are going to be manifested in this reality;

that's the Universe's job, not ours. I know that sounds odd, but nevertheless, our job is to be completely open by being completely joyous, thus vibrating at a sacred frequency, and the Universe takes it from there. Wringing our hands will cause what we want to go away from us, not come closer. The more joy we create, the more fulfillment will flow toward us now.

We can study all the reasons why things do not come our way and why we still feel disconnected from our own Higher Self, our love, our joy, our Deity. Using a key called joy/love causes one to switch to high frequency. The instant we see ourselves as we really are is the second we see we are in complete control of our lives; we are not just filled with love but we are love. Like the Goddess, we are and have enough love to supply energy that spins our Milky Way in perfect orbit. The Source is just like us; she is a giver. She is the mother that continues to birth all we need; she is eternal birth, like us. The Source supplies everything we need to live the life we choose to live. We are strong because she is.

One of the most important lessons is knowing how to choose our feelings carefully and with purpose. It is interesting that some cultures look down on feelings and emotions to the point that anyone exhibiting such behavior is ridiculed, or at least marginalized. To our detriment, we are told to control our emotions and hide our feelings. Now, no one is saying to be a raving emotional maniac; instead I am talking about having a strong sense of purpose; I'm talking about passion. Along with actions, we are able to deliberately choose strong emotions to make things happen.

We must remember to choose what we want in our lives, not what we don't want! Emotions are a good thing. "Feelings" are our inner guidance system. Our guidance system lets us know what we do not want or need, while passion propels us forward.

It is a huge waste of time to deliberately choose a thought that causes us to feel "bad." The person who has uncontrollable negative thoughts will attract the same misery to herself. I know these are harsh words, yet it is self-evident that it is our choice to reject or embrace such low-vibration frequencies.

One of the popular excuses is, "I have no control over what is happening to me." Yet this person usually has nonstop negative thinking and truly feels they have no options left and no control over their life or their thoughts. In fact, some will say just that: "I can't control my thoughts." They have given up their control and think it's not their fault, that nothing is their fault. And the possibility of choosing to control negative thoughts is foreign to them.

This negative person allows life to be shaped by ever-shifting circumstances, everything outside their self. Decisions indeed need to be made, but we must not allow our life to be overtaken by them. If you know a person like this, just love them. Just show them love and joy in your own way; that's all you can do. We cannot make them be any different. It is they who must see for themselves. As we identify all our aspects, all our sources, and see how we receive from all our helpers, we deliberately, with eyes wide open, begin to construct the most amazing life. We alter our worn-out beliefs, shifting to the concept that we alone form our lives; we alone choose to move with happiness in all its forms.

Happiness is the biggest key in our treasure chest. It is not natural to be unhappy or negative. Imagine how you feel after listening to a negative person speak or when you have a bad day and choose negative thoughts. Does it make the day better or worse? One negative thought begets another negative thought, and a slippery slope becomes steeper and steeper and more difficult to climb. Negative thoughts serve nothing and no one. A negative thought lowers our vibration frequencies and is only aligned with the base social consciousness and the ego-centered mind, which only begets more of the same garbage.

Yes, it is difficult to choose happiness at times. Everyone has a bad day or even a bad year. Everyone experiences sadness when a loved one has passed to the other side. In those times, we rest in the best way that helps to mend our wounds. One does not need to go find happiness because it resides inside us, at this moment, even in the middle of hardship. One does not find joy, because this is what we are.

Commit to living big, commit to living happy, and watch how we change the world and how we receive information, how we present information from within us. Commit to living happy; the view is much nicer here and the reception much clearer. Yes, there are days to weep, yet know our loving Source within will show herself by providing healing through every teardrop.

Dreaming Resources

Meditation #1

As you enter a meditative state, contemplate these meditation prompts:

- Our belief systems start as tiny seeds, planted and nurtured by our every wish, our very core thoughts. The farmer knows a seed must first be buried before he can reap his harvest.

- Nothing has come to us from outside us—ever.
- Do not focus on what you do not want, because you will receive more of the same.
- Be gentle with your lower self; love it back into the love and joy that are you.
- Our desires never come when we have not made a place for them and us to stand.
- We are Deity's receptors.
- Consider "asking" and "receiving" the same action. We receive what we are. When we become love, we attract love. "Love thy Self."

Common Questions for a Sea Priestess

If what I'm thinking is "not me," then what is doing my thinking for me?

It is only the base social consciousness, trained within an inch of its life and beaten down, or ego-centered thinker. We are more than the thinker, much more; our mind is much brighter than that. Our Divine Mind can connect to everything.

What do I do when I find myself complaining? Is this my lower self?

Yes. However, this incessant excuse maker will become a distant voice as you focus on hearing your Higher Self's voice and begin to realize your connection to Source. If you are too busy helping people, animals, plants, etc., you don't have time to be negative.

At this point in time, your mind should be having a fight with itself. It is a very good thing, because you are beginning to see your two selves—one working on the lower plane that needs to be untrained and the other on a higher plane that is ready to dance and sing with you, Sea Priestess. Pay attention to your feelings when each thought speaks to you. Stand back, watching as you identify how you feel.

This little exercise identifies which self is speaking and also identifies if you are doing what you want to do in life. Listen to your guidance system. How do you feel? Choose! If you are feeling "bad" consistently, then you are not doing what you are supposed to do with your life. You are not in the center of your purpose.

The lower self, ego-centered, base social consciousness always leaves you "less than" and needy. Select which self you will work with for the rest of your life. No matter how many reasons your lower self gives to stay within all its limitations, choose to completely feel, to open your eyes, and to live differently from how you have in the past.

One of the many reasons why it's important to identify the two selves is so that when one of your guides speaks to you, or Deity speaks, or you receive an inspired thought—that great idea—you will know who is speaking and no longer second-guess yourself. If you do second-guess yourself, you already know that your lower self just spoke. Identifying the little, complaining chatterbox is an immense step forward. Yes, it is entertaining at times, but keep it to small doses.

Why do I believe that I am not enough?

It is most difficult to believe that you are enough when it is the very opposite of what you have been trained to believe. Even commercials validate that you are not good enough, just so that a mere product may be sold! It is an untruth that many believe they need the newest thing to be happy. Sustaining happiness is never found within a thing.

Why is dreaming important?

Dreams reveal to us a snapshot of how and where we think—out of either fear or love, from either our Higher Self or lower self. The wish list shows us how we feel about our life, plus how we think we were created. All of these help us know thy Self.

You don't know what I have been through. I just can't "get" happy.

It is the ego-centered mind that makes simple truths so overly complicated. Happiness is the key to gaining our desires. Happiness produces results, just like negativity produces results. If more people knew that happiness is not a silly feeling but a grand key to gain a full life, everyone would be living in it. We have been trained to think that happiness is just a result, not the cause or a being. Some think that happiness is something we go find—out there. Untraining happiness is a natural force to bring our passions to us, not the other way around. We are happiness.

Exercise #1

The Wish/Dream List

In the last chapter, you wrote twenty-five wishes and twenty-five negatives. By writing these two lists, you now have a clearer picture of yourself. This list is not meant to be used to make you feel lesser; it simply reveals what is important to you. This list also reveals your shadows. Pull your wish list out and consider all the following questions.

1. As you read your twenty-five wishes, from where were you thinking? Your Higher Self or your lower self? Can you begin to sense the difference as you move through each list?

2. Go back and reconsider every wish. Are there any you want to change? If so, change them, keeping the original in sight for future reference.

3. Which wishes cause you to feel sad or hopeless?

4. Are there any wishes that come from fear, shame, or insecurity? Mark them.

5. Have you ever experienced pure joy? If the answer is yes, which wish reflects that moment?

6. Are there other feelings you are experiencing when considering your wishes?

7. Do most of the wishes go to the negative side? How many? For example, a negative wish might be: I wish I never see a particular person again. I wish I weren't bald, or short, etc.

8. Count how many wishes are "people" related.

9. Count how many wishes are "thing" related.

10. Count how many wishes are "event" related.

11. Count how many wishes are "experience" related.

12. Count how many wishes are related to you.

13. Count how many are Spirit related.

14. Count how many are "consumer" related.

15. Count how many are "need" related.

16. Did any wish cause you pure emotion—either negative or positive?

17. How difficult was it to write your wishes?

18. Are you surprised by anything on your list?

19. Do you see a pattern? For example, do you see more people-related wishes or thing-related wishes?

20. Was there a wish that you didn't dare to dream? If so, write it down and begin making plans to receive that wish. Just because the lower-self vibrations and base social consciousness tag team has beaten big dreams out of you, do not listen when they give you doubt. Their favorite words are guilt, shame, fear, unworthiness, selfishness, and undeserving, which are shadows.

Exercise #2

Identifying Lower and Higher Thinking

Say to your complaining thinker/self this: "I identify you as my lower thinker. What do you think about that?" And see what that thinker does.

This exercise will confirm to you that indeed you have two selves/thinkers. Your lower self is not "bad," it just needs to be retrained to agree with your Higher Self.

Exercise #3

Pick one wish on your list and do one thing today to get you closer to your dream. Then tomorrow, do one more thing to get you closer to your dream. Continue doing one thing per day until you have your dream. Do not pick an easy wish. Pick a big wish for yourself, because as you come closer to your wish, there are many wonderful lessons through your journey. Make sure it is your vision, not someone else's vision. Identify self-sabotaging behavior and curtail it.

⁕ 4 ⁕

Running with the Moon

Do not believe in what you have heard. . . . After observation and analysis, when it agrees with reason and is conducive to good and benefit of one and all, then accept it and live up to it.

—Gautama Buddha

As Sea Priestesses, we are actively listening to individuals in need, never judging as we work on our own shadows. Almost every problem originates from a place of not knowing the unbridled strengths we possess, not knowing we already have the answers within, not knowing who we are or how we operate, not knowing we have been taught subliminally or directly from the very first second we entered this plane to pull the plug on our own magnificence. We have been taught for centuries that we are our problems. We have been taught to define ourselves by our problems. We have been taught to listen to others first before we listen to our own Higher Self.

First we need to listen to our own Higher Self before we consider anything outside ourselves; if the concept feels right with our own guidance system and we have done due diligence with the information, we then can consider the information delivered. Just because someone says something does not make it your reality. It must line up with your sensibilities, not someone else's.

Some of us have been taught that to solve our problems, we must talk about our problems for months, for years, for decades, for our entire life, always focusing on the problem and never moving away from it or replacing it with a solution or a big, meaningful life. Have you ever noticed that a busy person has more time to do many activities, while a sedentary person who does almost nothing never has enough time to do anything?

This scenario also works when living with problems. The person who always defines everything by what is wrong accomplishes little, because they think their work is to be a fruit inspector instead of growing new fruit. But an individual who is solution-oriented accomplishes much. Everyone has a choice to live their life the way they see fit. However, if a person is always in hot water, always and forever has problems, and tries to pull you into their orbit, please think twice. There are times to help and times to step back and not enter another's nightmare.

As an adult, you have the capacity to see when to help up close or help from afar, depending on the circumstances and how often an individual ends up with problems. Basically, is there a problem pattern? Sometimes individuals can receive more help if we stay distant and do not enable them. Let them know they are loved, but you need to protect your own sanity, your own life, your own energy, your own time.

Thinking and talking about a problem incessantly, day after day, only attracts more of the same problem and prevents some people from ever getting out of the rut that seems to be their reality. The question then is, can you stop? These sad souls may think they can stop, yet do they want to stop? If they do not want to stop, there is no judgment there; just decide to make choices regarding your own life and how this individual can be part of your life or not.

Remember, we create our own reality, so let us take responsibility for our own behavior. If you think life is a never-ending crisis, you wake up each morning saying, "What awful thing is going to overtake me today?" Now because this is what you are creating, the same type of people and situations will be attracted to you. Everything in your reality will say yes to your most consistent thoughts. Then you might think that everyone lives this way, but indeed they do not. Life is not a continual crisis for many.

Once again, it is we who create our reality and it is we who confirm everything we believe is true by bringing more individuals into our lives just like us. Yes, we need to express to another human being, from time to time, that we are having difficulty. Everyone experiences sadness in their life, but not every single month! If an individual desires to step out of his nightmare, he has the capacity to do so.

We have all met individuals who have had heart-wrenching sadness in their life or conditions that made life more difficult; however, their personality is optimistic, positive, and when asked, they say they live in happiness and are grateful for what little they have. They focus on living and their solutions, not the problem—and they find a way to be happy. They choose to be happy. Yes, it is difficult to focus on a solution when we are going through a crisis. That's why friends, tradition, and family are so important; they are our support groups, and they can help us walk through the fire. Sometimes, as we move through the flames of crisis we cannot see through the smoke. Our support groups and our inner Sources will guide us through the thick smoke.

If we know we are pure magic, then we are pure magic in action and form. We are energy made of love, a living ritual ceremony. We operate and send our magic out through high-frequency vibrations found in joy and love. We send our focused energy out through electromagnetic waves, or what I like to call them, "electromagic" waves. That is how we operate almost every single day. That is how magic operates every single day. That is how we manifest our reality—through what we believe plus energy plus our deep-seated emotions cast out onto the World Ocean. Is it easy? Most of the time, no.

As a Sea Priestess, it is under our charge to help all who have an open heart and ear to remember who they are and how they operate. Once folks operate in magical terms, they see what they are, and Spirit teaches the other lessons. We are helping people remember that they are "Water Walkers." We are helping people tap into their own power, trusting their own strengths. We are helping them run with the moon. We are helping them to remember they are Divine, transmuting negatives into moon-white water. There are times when some negatives need to be completely turned away to move forward, while we can turn other negatives into opportunities. There are yet other negatives that cause imbalance, which is good because it helps us move away from that initial negative.

Focus on all the goodness this life offers. When we begin to see goodness, we are able to see more goodness.

When our focus is on good, more good comes into our lives. Find positive individuals, events, and experiences, as these show that life is not against us; life is for us, even when it is time to transition once again. You will receive from the Universe the measure you think you are worth, not a single thing more, because the Universe always agrees with you. See yourself as a boundless ocean, an incredibly valuable white-moon runner, because that is what you are.

You may ask, "What does that mean?" It means you are equipped to enter the waters and practice how to run with the moon. You are filled with like-minded water that is beckoning you to practice your Sea Priestess rights and forgotten skills. All Sea Priestesses say, "First, meet us in your dreams and love us, because we loved you first. This is our foundation."

Sea Priestesses do not tell others what to do or how to live; only you can make those difficult choices. As Sea Priestesses, we are learning to actively change our vibrations through our lives. We are learning to raise our vibrations with meaningful action through joy, actively and consistently selecting the positive side of life, even in the midst of baneful influences.

If

"If": what a tiny, seemingly innocent word on the surface. It is only letting us know why we cannot accomplish a task or experience, an event or emotion. It is only trying to clarify why we cannot accomplish what we desire or need. The word "if" is only telling us what "reality" really is. "If" is the most important word ever spoken by humankind, because there is always a perceived condition attached to it.

Individuals use "if" many times in discussions, dozens and dozens of times, to reason certain activities or desires away. It is the single untruth that stops a person from doing anything. It stops people from living to their fullest potential. "If" stops people from ever receiving emotional support for themselves and others. When a task or dream is finally accomplished, "if" never leaves people satisfied.

Individuals who have never felt love or success, but instead felt lack, cling to "if" as if it were some kind of safety device. Every so called "if" does not mean it is a good excuse to wait. Some ifs are good, while others are just another life stopper. Many individuals find it difficult to feel the emotion joy, the most important key to positive manifestation, because this insidious culprit, named "if," causes lack of feeling and is a life stopper.

Positive Beliefs versus Control Tactics

What if you are the moon, you are a Water Walker, you are a star—these are just some of the things you are. You are spectacularly brilliant. You are blindingly beautiful. You are all that is. You are loved beyond measure. You were created to play among the stars. You are the answer. You are happiness.

We have been trained to believe that we are none of those attributes, which is a colossal untruth. The most difficult task of unteaching us back to the beginning is to stop believing and living untruths and to start believing that the previous affirmations are indeed true. And when we live in truth, we live running with the moon. Sea Priestesses go one step further and prove each one of these precepts to themselves by operating in each truth.

By living in each truth, the Source will make your waters crystal clear, your purposes crystal clear. The

Source will show you, through you, that it is time to wake up and live your life as if you are important to the world, because that is an immense truth. If it were not true, you would not be here within this reality system. You, too, were and are authors of this story.

So many precious people sleepwalk through life, kept from their sacredness and purposes. Hindrances need not stop us in our tracks. It can be as small as "doubt" within us or a single thought that stops us. Doubt has been trained into us, and it is the number-one stall tactic and life thief. If we focus on doubt, we will spend our time in the land of the low-frequency, base social–consciousness mind; this results in the same old muddled results and control tactics of others.

These obstructions' main purpose is to hide our own purposes, our own strength, how we operate. The first example is those individuals who say they have the "answer." They claim that all we need to do is learn from them or their organization, only to find out that they or their doctrine have made people feel "less than" and reliant on them. If you ever run across a teacher who makes you feel this way, or informs you that there is only one way, run in the other direction.

Leaders from distant ages to the present still use this control tactic to cause people to think they need to be validated by someone else outside themselves, and then withhold validation, which is cruel, to say the least. People are trained to wait to receive permission to be great or are trained to be followers.

This model is being replaced by a new model. A model that says, "Everyone is equal and complete and just needs a little guidance to regain their full strength, to not give their power away to another. Everyone has a voice." And that little guidance essentially is saying that you have been trained to be something unnatural; now untrain and find out for yourself your answers and how you operate. What we have within our own being will fill our life; just a little encouragement and loving support is needed from time to time.

Some people have been taught that a "void" needs to be filled by all manner of things so that one may feel complete. I am honored and glad to say it is just another control tactic the world uses to keep us from operating our own lives, to keep us tied down to limiting dogma and doctrine.

The truth is that there is a void. The truth is that the void is a good place, a wondrous place. The truth is it does not need anything; it most certainly does not need to be filled. The truth is quite the opposite; the void is already filled to the brim with pure joy, pure love, pure inspiration, and all your treasures. The truth is there is no need to fill something that is already fully complete to serve you. Swirling, life-giving water spirals are found in the void, waiting to be more utilized by you. Yes there is a void, and it should be celebrated; the void fills you.

The void is absent of "need." Need was created outside us to make us doubt our own worth. How disgusting is that! All this time we have been trying to fill something that has nothing to do with need. The void is a place to embrace, a place to dive into head first. Dive into the void; it will embrace you. Some call the void Goddess; we call her Sea Priestess. Now that you have become more aware of your void, dive into the deep end and find out for yourself.

Goddess lives in eternity through the waters, easily accessible to us; we, too, live inside eternity.

Another control tactic is when we are not deemed to be as important as celebrities, presidents, doctors, the government, spiritual leaders, and so on. We are indirectly informed that we are regular, that we are not special, which is a tremendous untruth. This divisive tactic indirectly tells us what we need to do, what we need to have, where we need to move to, and how we need to think to be deemed important. I am pleased to report that no one—I repeat, no one—is more valid or important than you; no one for any reason. Please believe and live in this statement; it will help you find your true voice.

You are just as important as the scientist or the king. You are just as important as your spiritual leader. If you believed that tenet, you would dance for joy and laugh uncontrollably, knowing all is well. Deity needs everyone to create this story on this reality plane. We are taught we need Deity to flourish, and we are taught to live in need. The second we believe we are magnificence wrapped in pure love and joy is the second we wake up and see things as they really are and that nothing is against us or holding us back except for ourselves.

We are here to see and experience, to explore all that we really are. We are here to learn how we operate within this system. I can say with all certainty that you are just as important, needed, and brilliant as anyone on this earth. If you do not believe this statement, ask the many Holy Ones who have been sent to be with you. Begin to live as if you are a star, because you are.

Happiness has nothing to do with anyone or anything beyond us. Yet happiness is enhanced by generously sharing it with the world around us. When we remove false needs, wants also disappear. Wants are another control tactic used to shape our beliefs, a "Madison Avenue" tactic used to sell us a false sense of need. Madison Avenue creates a need by informing us that we have a need and, miracle among miracles, Madison Avenue has the solution—with a hefty financial price attached. This tactic is designed to cause us to become consumers, because we are told we "need" something and we need to buy it—right now. Once again, our happiness relies on a "needed" thing or concept outside ourselves. We did not know we needed that item, until the market told us we needed it!

When the holidays roll around, we hear the reporters judging the holiday spirit by the profits the stores make, all the while being reminded that the real gifts are not in the stores. You are the gift! It is you who is the gift that is needed, not the other way around.

It takes much strength and clarity to reject all these control tactics and life stoppers. It takes strength to remove all these untruths. It takes strength to not allow any person or group to rob your life, your joy, your purposes, your experiences. It takes strength to say "No!" to all those around you who are trying to drag you into their belief systems, into their nightmare. Some people live in another's nightmare for years by trying to help but with no results in sight.

It takes strength to walk away from ego-centered, negative personalities. To walk away from drama is to walk toward the big life that has been waiting for you. If you happen to have family members who have strong negative tendencies, please do not judge them; but know that your life must be protected from their habitual negative behavior. Deciding to live big has a cost, yet so does living helplessly. Choose the way you want to live, nullifying anything that interrupts your light. Do not allow anyone to influence your vision—it is your vision! This is your life.

Beautiful people, you are just as important as anyone from any time. Please consider making this precept part of your belief system. Please plug into the Divine Mind that liberates. When illumination occurs, doubt dissolves, and the Higher Self says, "Welcome to the light, welcome to your brilliant life." Learn to hear your Higher Self; it adores you. It will never cast a shadow over your life but will illuminate you from within. All of this is doable and attainable with sincere practice.

Happiness is within our reach as we align our new belief systems with what we really desire, accompanying it with practical work, laying down all self-doubt. It is a pure, unadulterated waste of time to be walking in doubt. The notion of doubt brings us nothing but pain and more doubt. Let us return to happiness. It takes strength to return to our inherent right that is happiness.

Running with the Moon Resources

Meditation #1

While in your daily meditation, contemplate the following prompt:

I see myself as an ordinary individual, walking through this life quietly, helping others work on boundless lives.

Meditation #2

Sea Mother Meditation

To prepare for this meditation, see a water plant of your choice in your mind's eye. It can be a plant that lives under the water line, above the water line, or along the shoreline in the soil.

All land plants can be used for any healing or success rite or working. All underwater plants, such as kelp and seaweed, can be used for purification rites as well as self-awareness meditations.

1. Release your mind by seeing your water plant grazing your entire body, starting from the crown of your head to the bottom of your feet.

2. Now ground yourself by seeing this same water plant take root in your feet, then see it take root into the ground. Feel the root grow deeper until you feel its roots hit water below the earth.

3. Center yourself by seeing this living spring travel quickly upward through the water plant's roots, continuing to flow upward through your entire body, seeing this water flooding your entire being and beyond.

4. Within this living spring enter stillness.

5. Invoke and welcome your master teacher spirit guide.

6. Request your master teacher to lead you to your Sea Mother.

7. As you travel to the sea, notice what you change into under the sea or if you change at all.

8. You are now deep within the ocean and swiftly going deeper. As you journey deeper under the sea, you pass caves and mountains; you are quickly swept into the ocean's heart and suddenly arrive near your Sea Mother.

9. Approach her, climb upon her, rest on her as she engulfs you with her loving arms. Allow her to heal you, allow her to speak to you; she will inform you

where to rest upon her. Just rest as she pours her love over and through you. Just be still, just rest, so that you may Be.

10. At this point in time, stay here as long as needed; bathe in her presence, her heart. You do not need to figure out anything, just allow her to minister to you. Allow yourself to be healed, treasured, nurtured, cherished; allow yourself to come alive. Allow yourself to receive her communication.

11. When you are ready to return to your physical body, leave the plant you chose to bring you here as an offering to the Sea Mother. Place the water plant anywhere that feels right. After you place your plant, notice the other offerings left around the Mother of the Sea. Depending on your comfort level, allow your master teacher to return you to your physical body, or return on your own with intent and breath, or allow Mother Sea to send you back to this reality system. Just know that by willing yourself back, you are back. Slowly open your eyes when you are ready.

12. Now that you have returned fully into your physical body, release, ground, and center once more, repeating the earlier steps in reverse.

After the meditation, consider and interpret what the Sea Mother conveyed to you. How did she transmit her communication to you? If this was your first time, know that you are stronger and brighter now than you were before this journey.

The moon runs the water as we run with the moon!

Common Questions for a Sea Priestess

What if no one sees or responds to my growth?

Only you need to see your growth. Yet know if you change, so will everything around you.

Exercise #1

Flip It Again and Again!

This is a fun, life-affirming exercise to help you identify how easy it is to flip your thoughts.

Get a sheet of paper, or something that serves as a writing surface, and pen. Write fifteen negatives about your life. Once you have finished with this list, go down the list and flip each one by writing a positive statement; write an active solution next to the negative statement. Read each of your negative statements and "flip " them into positives. As you read the rewritten statements, allow yourself to *feel* the negative change into a positive. No excuses! No stall tactics!

Start with a single negative, then purposely and deliberately choose to feel joy about this single item on the list. I see how individuals love this assignment and utilize it as a magical tool for their life. In fact, they try to come up with more negatives so that they can flip them to action-oriented positives, coming up with all kinds of innovative ways to transmute the negatives to positives. This is the time when people begin to get a little glimmer of how magnificent they are and how their negatives, their shadows, are in their hands to change into happiness or manifestation. They begin to see the positive already done, because it is.

When you move toward a solution, water wisdom comes. When you change, everything changes around you, just like water wisdom. It is not enough to decide to take action to reveal water consciousness through you; it is in the action where water consciousness resides.

Exercise #2

Each Answer Is Where You Are Going

If you truly believed that you are brilliant, that you are an important part of this grand experiment, that you are the answer, how would you feel?

How would you live?

How would you respond to toxic or negative individuals? On what would you focus? Would you still embrace false needs? Would you wait, patiently, to be validated by things or individuals outside yourself? Would your goals, dreams, and prayers change? Each answer is where you are going.

… 5 …

Some Reasons Why We Disconnect

As you teach so will you learn. If that is true, and it is true indeed, do not forget that what you teach is teaching you.
—A *Course in Miracles*

We chose the experiences we wanted to live in this life before we showed up on this planet. We choose what we want to experience every minute of every day. There are many narratives we have believed about humans, most designed to set up a barrier between you and your real water consciousness. Let us discuss a few tools and barriers.

For some, this truth is too great to handle and is totally rejected; it is too much of a burden to regain responsibility for their own light. Many are ready to live in the full light and take responsibility for their own life. They are ready to forge on and be part of this great evolution that is taking place at this moment. Many are, indeed, ready to cut the strings of a fear-based life and fly to new heights, experiencing life in a new, magical way. To experience life is why we are here.

Some of us find it difficult to dream big—for good reasons. For the first years of our lives, we were told in many ways and by many individuals to second-guess ourselves. This was our first disconnect. Of course, no one ever used those words; however, the training and purpose were still accomplished. As beautiful beings, some of us are covered with many layers of doubt, and we become disconnected, first from Self, then from all our helpers, causing our own feelings to become foreign to us. We soon forget our purpose in this life!

Many of us are afraid to succeed and will do everything possible to sabotage our every effort at every turn. To keep this disconnect, some fully participate in self-sabotage. There are many reasons why people self-sabotage. We must begin to identify our self-made sabotage tactics, seeing them for what they really are, and move on. There is an old saying that I will purposely paraphrase, "Do not do what you have done in the past, because you will get the same thing that you do not want."

Then there are others of us who do not know what we want or even need; this is a colossal disconnect from self-experiencing this life and connecting to eternity. The Universe asks, "What do you need?" The whys are no longer important. Do not allow the past to fence you in any longer. Do not allow the present to trance you into sleep any longer. Do not allow fear of "what if" to freeze your future from you. Only focus on what your needs are and what you passionately desire.

At this moment, after listening to these words in your mind, for some, self-doubt and fear will rush into your thoughts. Do not listen to these thoughts, for they are not the real you but only the trained mind reacting. Allow your Higher Self to react, the highest you.

Good results will appear as you begin to feel lighter and brighter. If shifting is difficult for you, then allow these self-sabotaging thoughts to drift in and then drift away; or tell them, "I will consider 'that' later; at the moment I am busy figuring out what I need, what I am." You will be amazed how these thoughts will behave.

Do not focus on lack, because you will only receive more of the same. Do not focus on what other individuals need to do to meet your standards, because you will only receive more people who will need to meet your standards. Do you see the cycle that begins and ends with its source? Have you ever noticed the same "negative" thing happens over and over in your life?

Many of us keep drawing the "negative" thing, event, or person to us by our own trained thoughts, our own "negative" vibrations. The Universe only matches and gives what we send out. Some folks focus on what is not wanted and keep getting more of the same thing. In fact, if we asked a group of people what they did not want, the group would not have any trouble coming up with dozens and dozens of things, people, and events they do not want.

If we then ask them, "What do you want?" some of them would still answer in the negative! Example: "What I really want in my life is not to have so many bills," or "I do not want to be sick any longer." Those are still negative statements! Do it this way: say out loud both of those statements to yourself. How did each statement make you feel? That feeling is low vibrational, connected to other low-vibrational energy.

The Universe generously listens, agrees with, and reacts to your energies, your feelings, your reality that you create. You create your events. You create you. You teach you. This is good news, knowing that the Universe agrees with you and ensures that you learn the lessons you have chosen to learn in the moment. Sometimes loss is experienced before gain is seen. Sometimes darkness is experienced to glean light and vice versa.

Everything you desire, receive, or learn will not only change you, it will also help everyone around you, including all your selves. The domino effect begins with you. First you are changed, then the people around you, then your community, thus your nation, then the world and beyond. The possibilities are endless; you are endless.

Many of us know what we want but choose to search for validation to do what we want. This is just a control tactic. We have been taught to wait until someone validates our life and no one does; this tactic works only if we allow it to work. On the surface, it seems sensible that we wait our turn to live our lives. That, too, is a crazy statement but sadly true for too many beautiful individuals. Do not allow this control tactic to stop you any longer; go out and live big! When naysayers say, "You cannot do that," say, "Oh, yes I can; watch me!"

Still others are just beginning to learn how to work with energy, to invoke what they want to accomplish in this life. Yet know that we need not be anything to be happy. One way to begin working with "joy" energy is to first experience joy to its fullest, by any means you choose so long as it is not harming anyone nor is it illegal. Choose to experience joy energy for five seconds a day, then ten seconds, then fifteen seconds, until you can hold pure bliss within your being for thirty seconds at will all throughout the day. Watch what comes rushing into your life, time and time again!

Next begin to focus all that wondrous joy toward a specific goal for thirty seconds a day. Yes, it will be a forced thing in the beginning; however, soon this will become part of your thought process. Plus this exercise kick-starts something that is rightfully ours. After a while, joy will not feel forced and can be switched on in a snap! Choose to be happy all day. That might sound impossible for some because of our training. If you feel that is the case for you, then choose to be happy for half a day. Do not wait one more second to be validated by anyone before you can be happy. Our happiness is no one's responsibility but ours. We will still experience loss in our life, except this time we know our heart is supported by our inner sense of peace.

Identify what brings bliss into your life, but first, get out there into the world and find out about life's possibilities. Focus on what brings happiness to you, which is you. See yourself already having it, because you do. First be happy, then happiness will follow you; not vice versa!

The Universe plugs into your joyful high vibrations, causing a joyful birth into this big life. Do not wait to find something that makes you happy. Be happy this very moment! Start now. Deliberately feel joy already within you. Do not pull the plug by doubting yourself. Then set up silly, fun things to do for the purpose of just laughing! A person said to me, in a Temple Gathering, "I guess we got off the track tonight with all of us laughing our heads off and all our silliness." I said, "No, we were right in the middle of the track!"

The Sea Priestess says: "I have lived a good life because I have lived in eternity and it is beautiful." Sea Priestesses many times choose to live quiet lives, or lives with physical challenges, to become transformative figures, sharing how to become self-enlightened and at ease with Self through self-correction. Of course, Sea Priestesses do not need to overcome a huge challenge to learn about enlightenment; we all chose how we were going to learn in this life. What we have or do not have is not relevant. When we talk about abundance, we are not talking about things or money.

We consider challenges as opportunities to show both our strengths and humor, so we laugh at a drop of a hat. We are not slaves to time, things, or fashion. However, we do have a specific, undeniable look.

Everything is considered spiritual to us, because we are spiritual. As we work with people, we help them gain knowledge of their own body, their own intelligence, their own self. As a Sea Priestess, we spiritually guide those who are ready to see eternity. And no, you cannot say, "Okay, I'm ready to be enlightened!" It does not work that way, for obvious reasons.

Some folks just want to have the "information" and nothing more, no genuine experience or service to the Great Work. And I cannot tell you what that looks like, only you can. There is nothing wrong with an information collector. When we speak to the person's "Higher Self," it does not matter if the person does not completely understand what is being communicated; the Higher Self understands and reacts with pure acknowledgment.

The amount of money in one's pocket does not make a person a success. We are interested in meaningful relationships that create growth for our personal evolution. We do not need to be anything to be something, we are already something. We are sometimes called Water

Mystics. We do not care what we are called. Success is not measured by most individuals' definition of success. Our success is immeasurable, for we are bigger than any common definition.

We all show up on this plane ready to express "All That Is" in our own way and within our own definition. One may reconsider the definition of success, and its benefits, if the definition of success does not benefit others' potential. So then, what is the point?

We are not measured by what we outwardly possess. We are not about "power" or politics. We have worked quietly for eons, planting crystal seeds of enlightenment, never limiting or holding anyone back. We believe everyone is ready to be awakened; enlightenment is reachable for everyone, not set aside for the "special" few. The only way to be found far from a Sea Priestess is by being an ego-centered person or one who speaks against loyalties and serenity. Yet we always know, those people, too, are already holy and whole; they just do not realize that beautiful truth yet.

We have never been interested in starting a new religion nor dogma. Eternity is bigger than any religion, and dogma is far from it. We are living in eternal birth. We are Sea Priestesses, hunting and calling forth all those who have already been trained in other lives, within the Sea Priestesses' Temple, within the Holy of Holies. This is a sacred hunt. Ancient memories are rising from the sea, giving us strength and vision to search the cosmic ocean. We move quietly in the deep, beyond the shadows, behind the light, uplifting others and bringing peace on the waters. We do not wait for a test or savior. We design our own tests, and we are champions. We know we are not the only ancient people who are now walking this earth. Everyone is an ancient thread tied through every ancestor here.

How do I know that I am a Sea Priestess? Look at your personality, look at you; what do you see? Do you see selflessness? Has anything changed? I do not need to reveal all the "signs" to everyone, because not everyone is a Sea Priestess, which is perfectly fine. Yet everyone is both ancient and newly birthed. This path is not for everyone. Everyone is connected to a family; everyone is already home! Sea Priestesses, among other things, are helping people to begin to see that everyone is capable of receiving all that *is*—everyone!

Spiritual truths are not just for those who breathe rarified air high on the Himalayas or have dozens of degrees; sea treasures are for everyone who has an open heart and mind. Or to say it another way, it does not matter what you do not have or what degrees you do not possess. We are all already healed, and we are all holy—every one of us. Though some live a life solely devoted to Source while making clay pots in India, others may be a store clerk, and others wear the robes of high priesthood—all are sacred. All are equally utilized to expand light, if their hearts are selfless and have no hidden self-agendas.

Have you noticed that spiritual leaders are different within this age? Are you blessed enough to be part of a group that is set up with the new group model? The new group model is one in which the leader strives to train and raise up as many leaders as possible. The new group model is not interested in having followers. It is interested in having light workers, leaders who have motives that are not about collecting people but guiding people to be good spiritual leaders. With this great change, as always, we remain within the water, only proving that the greatest truths are simple. The greatest truths are right in front of your face. The greatest truths are found beyond symbol. The greatest truths are spoken from one teachable, open-hearted person to another teachable, clear heart.

Identifying Your Disconnects Resources

Meditation #1

Run Confirmation

As you enter your meditation, reflect on these prompts:

- There is no space between me and Source, thus it is impossible to be disconnected from Source, disconnected from my Higher Self, disconnected from your my cosmic story.
- I will run to the light.
- I will take responsibility for my big beautiful life.
- I will live my life to the fullest.
- I will bless and see Deity in everything, as blessings follow me home.
- I accept the precept that Deity desires me to live in pure joy and expression.
- Through healing, I walk in joy! Follow the joy.

Do you feel an ancient memory coming to the sea's surface? Concentrate on the memory and allow the memory to be the bridge that helps you rediscover your infinite connection to Source.

Common Questions for a Sea Priestess

What if I do not know how to figure out what I want?

Your feelings are your gauge or guidance system. Your feelings are telling you what you need to remove from your life. Your feelings are telling you what you want. For example: If you feel joy when you think of an event, thing, or experience, that is what you want. What are you doing now? And how do you feel? You are telling yourself what you want.

If you feel miserable, tired (without cause), stressed, or nothingness, then that "thing" is not what you want. This sounds simple, but it is amazing how we avoid checking our own feelings every moment of the day. Most great truths are hiding right under our noses. People have told us to not pay attention to our feelings, that everyone lives in extreme stress. We are told that stress is "normal"; it is not. We are taught how to swim upstream all our lives, then die. We are told to not trust our own feelings. Give me a break! That reason makes no sense. Flip that reason and restate it.

Exercise #1

Use these steps to help you commune with your Higher Self and your inner guides:

1. Continue to commune with your Higher Self by believing that you can.

2. Continue to commune with your spirit guides.

3. Have fun.

4. Decide on one thing you want in life, and do one thing this week to start bringing it into your life. Do not talk about it; make it an actionable step toward a reasonable goal.

5. Start identifying self-sabotage activities and stop them. Just identifying a self-sabotaging tactic deflates its power over you almost immediately.

≈ 6 ≈

Move

You have nothing to do but to convince yourself of the truth which you desire to see manifested.
—Charles Haanel

Movement is first; movement is always first. As you may have noticed by now, I have not yet focused on "problems." We will continue to focus on everything beyond problems, so that we may discover that we are fully entering ever-expanding consciousness and movement, day by day becoming bigger, brighter, stronger, fuller, and clearer. Then, when we begin to discuss "problems," we will see our problems in an entirely new light. We will see our "problems" as only "weak ideas," fallible ideas that are only mirrors that interfere with one another. We will also see that most problems will have already been dissolved, while others dramatically diminished! Due to our ever-present focus on the Great Work.

Everything is a choice and choice is a mutable idea, controlled by us. Some people walk through their day numb, not feeling anything that is not in thriving mode, fluid mode filled with excitement. Some think negative thoughts all day long; that is not living. Some individuals think they are above others and nature; that, too, is not living. Some individuals receive information through their negative thoughts and not through all their senses and gifts; that's not living. Plus, if seen through a negative lens, they cannot see clearly what is right in front of them, let alone evaluate their own skills. Some individuals hear their own isolating reasoning, not willing to hear everything trying to teach them; that is not living. Some think that there is no need to receive what they do not understand nor consider adding to their life.

You may have heard those people say, "It has always been this way, so it is always going to be this way." Or you may have heard someone say, "Everyone is the same." Some think they have many problems; however, they do not. They only have one, and it will soon be seen as dust. Choose to say, "I will choose to live life with passion, entering the waters of love and drawing every good thing to my life and all humans and all that may enter this earth. The waters of compassion will heal as we evolve to meet our glory, thus healing it and us. I bring everything to me through joyful waters. I will use my tears to heal my deep wounds."

As we approach problems from the solution, or positive side, we have a clearer view of all shadows. Let me give you an example. Some say the only way to work on our shadows is to go into the dark; only there can we then see the light. A Sea Priestess does the opposite. She enters into light to see her shadow self, for only the light reveals clear, crisp shadows. Light shows shadows; darkness shows no shadows for the Sea Priestess. We choose the light by making choices that fit us. Not a ready-made, one-size-fits-all choice but a deliberate choice that can only be made by us as individuals.

The Sea Priestess says, "I give to you a gift. I give and make it completely your gift. Then the gift is almost immediately changed and made to be your gift, fashioned by your hands." By choosing life, we choose movement. As Sea Priestesses, our movements are filled with compassion, helping others to their pure essence so that they may walk in their Water Way, for, indeed, individuals commonly ask, "Which way shall I go?"

Your true Self says, "You are the way!" When we move to help others and ourselves, most of our problems disappear, because we are listening to Sea Priestess of the Goddess saying, "What do you want?" If we are overcome by problems, we must then become flexible, bendable, and moveable to avoid what has come our way. If we are stiff and unmoveable, we remain within our self-made "problems."

Today is the day to move closer to your work, your life, and away from the ego-based group consciousness of others' consumerism. The "everybody thinks this" consciousness is what we as Sea Priestesses are not, for we are independent thinkers, turning the big ego upside down and seeing the massive benefits of that movement. As critical thinkers, we do not wait to find out what we shall think nor wait for approval to live our lives. When we identify distractions, we are not saying they are "bad." But for this lesson, anything that stops or slows the process of discovering Self eventually becomes harmful, becoming frozen in the most generic sense within our lives.

It all comes down to choice; we move through life with every choice we make. We select every single minute of every single day to continue our connection—or not. Some choose to think garbage, day in and day out, and wonder why their life is miserable and filled with lack. Some of us have a difficult time believing we can actually change our lives, choosing to place invisible barriers constructed by our own hands, and some allow others to place us into small boxes, and we say "thank you" as the lid is placed over the box. We allow others to label us. At first glance, it seems to be a sensible thing to do, it seems to be the right box. At least that is what we are told; after all, that is how it has been for generations.

You have heard the statement, "Let us not expect too much, then we will not get hurt." We second-guess our own inspirational thoughts. We have the capability to see ourselves as the dancers we are. Some of us need to be given permission to see things differently, to be an independent mind (not the ego thinker) and to be connected to the universal, ever-fluid Ocean Mind. We are Divinity seeing through the eyes of a cosmic, ever-moving dancer. We have a tiny spark within us; as a reminder, we are the dancing spark within Goddess. Through our dance we change the world.

The Sea Goddess is waiting for our next move. She is waiting for our next dance. Still, some of us choose to use stall tactics—we talk the talk; however, we do not walk the talk (or shall I say dance the dance?). An example of this is when individuals say, "Okay, I understand the concept. I need to study it for a few months or years; I need to think about it a little longer. Then, maybe, I'll consider living big in the near future." Or "That is what I believe. I just have not had time to apply it to my life." You see where I am going with these general statements? They are very reasonable statements, but they are all stall tactics.

Why are some of us afraid to live our own life? Why are we afraid to dance for the sea? Becoming upset can also be a stall tactic. Go ahead and get angry if you must from time to time but move on and join your dance.

It is imperative to move on after being frustrated or getting angry about something or someone. There is nothing wrong with dealing with anger and drama every once in a while. In fact, drama reveals to us of what we are made, and anger and drama can be motivators as well. We must quickly move away from such low-vibrational energy, or we will end up with the same negative situations, over and over and over again. We do not have enough time in this life to continually focus on negative circumstances and our watery skills at the same time, at least not for long, though we do try our best to accommodate both at times.

Of course, we need to deal with discord at times but not every week. By staying in strife, we are choosing to not have our needs or goals met. When we choose to live our lives to the fullest, dancing by the light of the moon, watch what happens. Choose happiness. That is right: happiness is a choice that already resides within us and is us. Sometimes we need to be spiritual warriors, moving through all manner of garbage, yet we know soon there will be quiet respite. If negativity had any benefits we would have seen them by now; thus it is a complete waste of time to choose to stay within negativity.

The universal Ocean Goddess is waiting to see your joy. She is waiting to hear your song. She is waiting to experience your dance. Some may say, "But what if I did not have the opportunity to choose happiness?" We always have the power of free will—always. The times when we feel we have no way out of a mess, that we have no one to turn to, are the times we choose to become spiritual warriors and believe in our own promise, in Ocean Goddess, in the Sea Priestesses that called us from the beginning.

We think we are trapped because we do not use the power of free will. Eternal victims feel they have no way out and no choices to make; they have been rendered helpless. Low-vibrational social consciousness rises again, trying to control us instead of us controlling it. We always have choices. Let us ask our spiritual guides to give us suggestions as we choose to generate what we want and what we do not want. We have a choice.

Start raising your vibrations through joyful dance. One must make the choice to move into and agree with vibrations that align with what you want. Feel it strongly; feel it! Dance bright vibrancy into your life. I have never met a sad dancer; maybe there is a reason for that. Do not beg for anything, because that is negativity. Once again, the Universe is listening to our frequency, waiting and asking, "What do you want?" It is your life. Choose to remove doubt, for it is a waste of time and slows everything down. Doubt is a low frequency that stalls everything.

When a problem enters your life, use it as a time to grow your potential; choose to expand your Goddess consciousness. Ask your Higher Self and all your helpers to reveal the options. Goddess will prepare the way for us, yet she will never do anything outside our focus, our vibration. Walk in inspired harmony with your pure light guiding you closer to who you really are—a Dancer of the Lighted Sea Goddess. In knowing, we have options. In knowing, we have freedom to dance. Go inside and listen to the many options available to us. There is never just one "right" answer.

Receive through the Water

It is no accident that the largest living organism on earth is underwater; the Great Barrier Reef moves with the moon and so do we. Fear not, because we lovingly embrace the call of the shadows, for we know we are of the bright, white moon and the sun herself. Test each one of these world views under the water; feel shadow symptoms move deep within us. The moon moves the waters on earth and inside us. The moon moves the Great Barrier Reef in Australia, where the reef and all life within it move with the moon. Allow the moon to move you and see that it already is moving you.

If you select an answer and start saying to yourself, "I can't do this; I am not good enough," that is the worst kind of violence against you. It is like punching yourself in the face over and over; in the end, you lose a little more of yourself. Even if others start making you become violent with yourself by saying, "You cannot do this because you are not good enough," even if it is just implied, run from them. It is time to make a choice to move, make a choice to connect.

Many indigenous tribes find their way, and shaman name, through trance dance. Ocean Goddess, moving you into rushing waters of life, waking you to see the light of eternity, moves you with your heartbeat. Our responsibility is to fully experience life so that the Goddess experiences and learns through our experiences. The Sea Priestess's shadows call in the night but can only be seen in full sunlight.

What are you? Depending on your age, culture, and your world view, you will decide how you answer that question. There is a shadow cast behind every one of these world views, and there is light at the center of each, revealing every shadow and every light value. Everything moves and is shaped by water and movement.

There's Something in the Water

That old question is sometimes asked jokingly, "Is there something in the water?" The reality is, it is we who are found in the water. All water is not the same, as we are not the same. There are some water places on earth that we, as humans, cannot even see let alone touch in the physical. As Sea Priestesses, we are capable of journeying to these sacred, hidden, seemingly undiscovered waters. One of our great tasks is to help heal the waters.

Connect to water by merging with it as one being. Listen for its messages and bring them back to meditate upon. Water needs to be healed by the Sea Priestesses and any other beings that belong to the water; in turn, the water desires to heal us, Father Earth, Mother Earth. We are one species within water. Water is mother and the sun, moon, and cosmic ocean.

Every water source truly has a different teaching. Every water source always starts with the same ancient chant, "I, I, I," in every breath and every statement we used to chant "I." Are we willing to see beyond the basic "I" chant? Because humanity has truly moved far past this elementary stage. The answer needs to be a resounding yes.

Sea Priestesses heal the water and not only learn from its recorded knowledge, we teach it, too. Providing sustenance to water is essential to everyone. It is our ancient recorder for all living things connected to Goddess. She is everything. Recorded knowledge, written by all formal and informal historians, brings up an interesting issue: recorded knowledge is not "history."

History would like us to believe in history, but it is woefully lacking in accuracy and depth and everyone's perception—not just that of the violent victor. History is always written by the victor, and, of course, the victor will discredit the so-called defeated. When history is written, it is written from a single, self-promoting prospective that will give so-called facts on how events happened. The fact is, any fact may be seen completely differently, depending on the gender, culture, education, age, religion, tradition, and so on of the person perceiving it.

If history's facts are questionable, then it is not history but yet another story. I am not saying not to study history. I am saying take history with a grain of salt and find out for yourself what really happened, if possible. Many times, all it takes is to put our intent out there and some information will be sent to us, from us, even if it is just reassuring us that we are on the right track.

Just think of us as recorders, because we are water; and because we are the water, the information comes from within. We can also go to that time period through journeying or astral travel. It is not natural for our own human history to be hidden from us; yet at this time, it is. All things purposely hidden will be uncovered one day through water, turning the world upside down. Or shall I say, right-side up again?

Now think about this: do we really think the cave persons were ignorant because they did not talk or invent reading? Do we think cave persons had nothing to pass on to their children? Do we really think those cave drawings were just primitive attempts at depicting how they hunted? Their children already saw how they hunted.

Cave drawings were not created to kill time. They were drawn because the drawings were much more than drawings. They had beautiful sacred meanings as well as practical applications, the best of both worlds. Cave persons had the natural talent of having one foot in each world. At one point, they knew that there was no need to take care of the dead, because they saw that no one died, just willingly transitioned from here to there. World Walkers, shamans, psychopomps, Sea Priestesses, and the others see both sides of practicality and spiritualism.

Some cavemen did not do anything special with a dead body. Then, as time passed, humankind decided to change their attitude toward the dead; an indication of this attitude change was when this species began laying flowers next to the dead. Some say this proves they were becoming more human; maybe yes, or maybe no. Sadly, death was a natural part of life for the caveman. They knew that the deceased did not go anywhere. Once people began to move away from nature and allowed themselves to be directed away from Source and Self, then they began to forget the story, the Source. Eternity was now considered far away; thus some began to honor their dead by placing flowers by them.

The memory of our species, from where we came and how we developed to this point, is what is in the water. We have lost much as we allowed ourselves to be taught by mere words. Yes, words are important to get to a certain distance. Yet words are a far less effective way to gain "knowing." As Sun Tah Oaness, a shaman, once said, "It is difficult to explain about enlightenment, because humans rely so heavily on words; it is like drying water off something using water."

That is why Pagans through the ages have utilized sacred art, dance, and nature to move into "knowing." All are capable of entering this now; we are the recorders because we are made of the waters and the stars.

It is humbling and comforting that Sea Priestesses are now making themselves known to us. My heart is filled with joy and gratitude as beautiful, strong, loving Sea Priestesses say, time and time again, "Here I am. What shall I do?" So I start everyone with shadow work, because I know it is easy for them, because they have few attachments to consumerism, materialism, or lower-vibrational control. I treat them with utter respect and love, because I know how important they are to *move* this great change forward. Like all devoted to the Great Work, no matter what they are called, they all have decided from the beginning to move to change and evolve as everyone is.

Movement Resources

Meditation #1

Consider these questions and prompts as you move through your daily meditation:

- Have you met life today?

- Have you met a Sea Priestess today? There is so much to see through the eyes of a whale, dolphin, and coral.

- It is we who see through the eyes of Deity.

- Choosing passion is true empowerment, the very force of the Universe.

- Moving in compassion is emerging with water's high vibration.

- Love problems away.

- Allow a negative thought to enter your mind, then choose to transmute it. Choose to change it, or it will change you. Let go of anything that stops you from living the life you want, and the whole world will be blessed.

- Raise your energy; intensely flow with dazzling joy. Move! Let us keep our focus off lack and move.

Common Questions for a Sea Priestess

How can I work with arrogant people and still live in joy?

If we run into a blatantly arrogant person, we have the choice to run in the other direction or at least love the person from afar. We always have two choices. Choose to focus on being ticked off, and that will only hinder us. Or choose to focus on our own dreams, for that's where our magic resides. We must control our thoughts, or they will control us.

Life is never about what the other guy is doing; it is about what you are vibrating out. Everything is created by our own deep, core emotions and beliefs. It is not our concern to change anyone; we only change our selves. There are times to diplomatically speak your mind; however, consider the cost, because someone always pays. When we speak our mind, we then need to forget it and move on to mastering our vibrations.

What are the benefits of being connected and moving?

It is the beginning of wisdom, hope, compassion, abundance, awaking to peace. It is the difference between swimming upstream or downstream!

Why is it so important to learn control or choice?

We create our wants and make them come true by what we generate and how we move; that is, if we choose to feel bad, we will receive the same bad things. If we choose to feel good about a bad situation, then better things will come. Choice has nothing to do with "trying." It is making strong movements and choices about your life, not the life down the street—*your* life.

Choosing to be negative, or even neutral, is a colossal waste of time. It will bring us what we already have and don't want more of, and we will continue to receive it until we actively choose to keep our vibrations high, becoming busy with good works for others. We are generators cranking out our existence by our strong or consistent emotions or thoughts. Yes, negative things come into our lives, at which point we deal with them quickly with wisdom and compassion, moving them out of the way.

Exercise #1

Red and Yellow Exercise

This exercise is a one-day assignment, but you may apply the exercise for longer if you choose. Obtain two stacks of small pieces of paper, one stack of red and one stack of yellow. The color red represents *stop* and the yellow color represents *slow* (stall). The red stack is for any thoughts, speech (others' and yours), events, people, or drama that *stop* you from working on you and your goals. This can be anything—any individual, any TV commercial, any activity that makes you feel badly or less than, anything that insults your sensibilities.

Identify them as such by pulling a sheet of red paper and writing what made you feel negative. This part of the exercise will make you stop and think how many times a day you are bombarded by junk that directly affects your movements and thoughts.

The yellow stack is for any thoughts that say, "I'll do that later"—any talk, events, people, or drama that stalls you. It's not necessarily a negative thing, but nevertheless it slows your progress. An example of this is watching too much television or doing anything too often. This is a stall tactic for living, unconsciously sabotaging your growth and hindering the things that you want in your life. Does the activity zone you out or make you feel numb? Then it is a stall tactic. Write each stall tactic on a small piece of yellow paper.

By the end of one day, or as long as you would like to do this experiment, you will have two piles of paper. Now count each pile. You will see in living color how you do not move by your choices. You made the choices; no one else did, just you. Ouch! Read every negative thing on every paper slip, then flip it and say (or use your own words): "I transmute this to a positive and will learn from this." Turn every negative thought on every slip of paper into a positive statement. Move every statement into a positive vibration or dance. You will see growth, plus you will be able to control your mind, not the other way around.

Here are some examples of flipping a negative. Keep in mind, these are only suggestions:

- Nobody likes me. *Flip it.* Everyone likes me! (Act as if everyone likes you and believe that everyone likes you.)

- I don't like where I work. *Flip it.* I see myself loving my work. I have so many wonderful things I can incorporate into my workplace to make it better.

- I never have enough. *Flip it.* I have more than enough.

The biggest flip helpers are gratefulness, love, allowing, compassion, passion, and removing blame.

I can hear someone saying, "Now this is silly. I don't need to write on papers every time something negative floats in my head, because that's all I would be doing all day!" If that is the case, guess who really needs to do this exercise?

Every thought is our choice. Stay away from the low-vibrational thinkers. If you do not know how to avoid the low-vibrational thinkers, just pull yourself back outside yourself and watch the social-conscious thinker. Just watch it. You will quickly see that you are not it, and you will know how to pull out of it. You are "being." Your senses and receiver are much bigger than your brain or body. Your true Self, or Higher Self, goes far beyond your body, and you possess infinite intelligence.

Who is watching the thinker? Who is the watcher or witness? How can we watch the thinker if we, in fact, are much more than the thinker? We have been taught to think our responses. However, to get plugged into the infinite, we need to *feel* our responses. We do not need words. Being is aware of itself. With watching comes empowerment. We can choose to move through feelings, through strong emotions to the astral.

Exercise #2

Meditate near the water. Be still; allow your Self to be fully present—no past, no future, just fully aware of is-ness. Go inward, not outward. Proclaim "I am Spirit."

7

Poisoned Waters

The body is the house for the thoughts or energies.
—Hawaiian proverb

Lost focus is one of the biggest dream thieves. We assume that all people are taught how to make plans, how to begin and travel a well-worn path, and how to finish or complete a goal. Maybe that assumption is incorrect; most individuals have not been taught to run to the finish line. I believe there is a direct connection to a person's ability to see themselves living with their dream and with what they have been taught. I believe some individuals carry with them beliefs that are truly not their own but have been given to them by others.

Magic is about the journey of self-exploration and improvement. Look behind the dreamless person, the one with no goals or interests in life, and you will discover a shadow called fear. This results in incomplete cycles within this person's life or borrowed beliefs from others. Normally, a person who leads their life by fear has a difficult time with commitment, thus it is easy to understand why this personality has a rough time staying the course or even seeing the course. Fear causes broken commitments, which causes disconnection every time.

There are times outside forces try to destroy our life by handing us their beliefs and their troubles. Times like these are most sad and most difficult to walk through. If you have ever had a crime committed against you, if you have suffered any loss, or if your body or mind is ravaged by a chronic disease, the higher intelligence within us is always there to guide us through these life storms. We will learn our lessons and move on, for we must move on to truly learn our lesson.

If we find ourselves in too much pain, we can ask if we could learn the lesson in a gentler manner. We decide what we want to experience before we enter this reality, and we can change our mind. Through no fault of our own, we will run into some difficult personalities that we will have to deal with; some personalities are so toxic, sucking all the life from everyone within their reach, that we must protect our life and our dreams from such poisoned waters.

We cannot help others, or even live our lives, if we are always dealing with a toxic personality. A toxic personality has a talent for creating drama every other week and thinks drama is normal. They even say, "Everyone has drama." Sure drama happens once in a while, but not every week! If drama occurs every week, you are or have a toxic personality in your life. This personality needs to be fed attention every waking moment, thus robbing everyone's joy, time, and energy; exhausting every one of all their energy and even money; always needing something yet never, ever being satisfied.

Another, more subtle toxic personality is someone who thinks they have the best ideas and thinks they should be the leader of any group. They make little passive-aggressive statements about the current leader for the purpose of slowly discrediting the leader. That personality almost never has any substantial training on how to lead; however, they still behave as if they are the "All-knowing One." No one desires to hear from a person who behaves this way, who does not respect everyone else's knowledge.

As a Sea Priestess, I only give recommendations. It is you who makes any decision on how to handle such personalities within your group. I only want you to live the happiest life you are able to, as a human and Sea Priestess; everyone is a leader, everyone is a teacher, everyone has much to offer humanity.

Maybe for the past several years you just have not had the time to accomplish what you want, and maybe you did not realize that all your time has been taken up by a toxic person or poisoned waters. It's something to consider, as you step into the deep end of the pool. Do not spend too much time on these personalities, because our focus is on Spirit, brightening our light so that it aligns with the missions we chose. I know that sounds harsh; however, it is we who lead our groups or lives, making difficult decisions, so that our main vision stays intact and our teachings evolve through loving.

It is our task to help guide others on a journey to self-improvement, to grow and remember that we are all here because of the Goddess loving us. Some leaders like to spend too much time with these toxic personalities, indirectly using them as great excuses for why their vision is not moving forward. These personalities can cut a group down to its knees if the group does not have a well-seasoned leader and the group members do not love and support one another, including the leader.

Poisoned waters can show up in many ways other than just in personalities; another way is to have everything taken from you. If you truly have a legitimate excuse to not capture your dream, or live big, I understand. Conversely, Steven Hawking, the genius of the twentieth century, did not use his debilitating condition to keep him from expressing himself. Once individuals realized that he could communicate through a computer, the world was changed by his brilliance; nothing kept him from moving forward.

Don Lewis, Chancellor of the Correllian Tradition, had a terrible accident that left him bedridden for approximately a year. Although he was in constant pain, he did not allow this tragedy to stop him from moving forward with the Correllian Tradition. It was during this time that he wrote most of the Degree writings for us. He knew then that he needed to write this knowledge, not for himself but for us. He looked into the future and saw us.

I also know another man who was homeless at the age of fifteen. He lived in a peach orchard in New Jersey, had no money, had nothing, but got himself up every day to go to school, where he struggled to read and write. Even though this boy was incredibly intelligent, no one could see how intelligent he was. Every day was a struggle, and he had a million legitimate excuses to not capture his dream or not go to school. He refused to take no for an answer and used what he had, which was utterly nothing but his thoughts, to slowly capture his dream.

Yes, you have every right to live any way you select; you can select nothing, just so long you select it and that is what you desire to be perfectly content. That is to be honored as well.

I am sure we have all heard these statements: "I tried everything and nothing works," "I can't finish that because . . . ," etc. There are some people who have this pattern within their lives: something almost happens, something is almost earned, something is almost gained, almost found, almost, almost, almost. This personality always starts with great intentions and great plans but soon begins to work against their own plans by collecting excuses as if they were their oxygen, literally collecting reasons to not reach their own self-made goal. This good person desires to reach the finish line, even while their words and actions say differently, but is left wondering why they lost focus along the way and cannot make those last steps to cross the line.

Yes, we all have bumps in the road. However, this person's road always has bumps. I call this life movement "incomplete cycles." A person who lives within incomplete cycles makes sure they have myriad barriers at the ready—before they even begin! This way, they can console themselves and others by saying, "I really wanted that dream, *but . . .*" and will pull out a trusty excuse. They will look at the excuse as if it were their original goal.

Out of nowhere, something happens! Something always happens! This personality believes everyone lives in incomplete cycles, but we do not. Sometimes, there are people within our lives who are toxic and may be a huge part of why we cannot achieve what we want or need in our life. We need to identify them, not judge them; just identify them and work around them. Now, if you have identified everyone in your life as toxic, then guess what? It is you who is toxic, not them.

Some excuse makers may intentionally utilize these toxic personalities to keep themselves hidden from life, remaining just an observer. The people with this issue almost always have different types of toxic people at their fingertips—the drama queen or king, the control freak, or the infamous Ms./Mr. Big Ego, a person who has an ego the size of Texas. This cast of characters is at the excuse maker's beck and call. The excuse maker must ask herself, "What do I really want? Do I want that education, that job, that house, that business, that relationship, that experience?" If the answer is a resounding yes, then allow nothing to push you off your path; consider roadblocks as stepping stones in your life.

It is your path and your roadblocks. The trick is knowing when to jump over, dive beneath, walk around, dissolve, or transmute the roadblock and make something that was meant to stop you become something that propels you forward toward your goal. You can remain friends with a drama queen or king, the control freak, or Mr. Big Ego, but do not get sucked into their reasoning, their drama, their grand plans, or their rules, because their vortex will cause you to be pushed aside and rendered helpless.

When dealing with these poisoned-water types, you will get pushed around—guaranteed. If you play with fire, you will get burned. Not them, you. Once you take a step back from toxic personalities, the fog will lift. It is now time to follow through with your plans; your plans are equally important. If you keep getting something you do not want, it is because you are focusing on what you do not want; you are focusing on poisoned waters. Look beyond what you have and see your goal in your hands.

Think Small

Think "I can take this one small step today." Then take one small step that will bring you closer to your dream.

We need to be untrained so that we can focus on one small thing a day.

It is untrue that dreams are unattainable; they are attainable if they come from you. We need more dreamers. There are "things" still unknown at this time, things that only dreamers can uncover. There are things that the world does not know we need yet. There are places that need to be discovered. There are species that are still hidden from us and need to be uncovered. So let us dream small, because sometimes we need to become small to see the big picture, before we can see the All.

Sometimes, when we discover the smallest part of something, we realize it is the smallest part that moves the larger parts. Uncovering the smallest parts unlocks our understanding of the largest part. Consider a small rudder that guides a large ship on the water. The way to gain all this is to finish your dream. Poisoned waters are just excuses or individuals we use as excuses. This means that we are fully capable of pouring fresh water into the poisoned water until all is healthy and clear again. The manner in which we keep our waters excuse-free is up to our discretion.

Dreams regarding Art

When talking about words, they are, in essence, symbols agreed upon by the culture utilizing them. Art, too, is a record of the past. In many pantheons, and in many times, where the enemy has destroyed all written records, it is art that tells the stories of a long-lost civilization. In those artworks, we see that humanity had many excuses but knew we were their future and left art to help us see how they lived and how they reached their dreams. We see them through art; they see us through our accomplished dreams.

Art works both ways. Art is a double-edged sword or a two-sided mirror. Art can be used as a spirit language that bypasses our thinking mind and directly opens communication both ways. Sometimes we think we have a specific question we would like answered. Then the Higher Self answers a completely different question! This is exciting because now we have yet another answer to ponder in meditation. Sacred art is a beautiful dance of ebb and flow, until everything flows into just one thing. Not two things but one thing, to the point at which we do not know if we or the Water is asking the question. This brings us back to the simple questions: What is being? Who is asking the question? Who is moving? Who is thinking?

Poisoned Water Resources

Meditation #1

Consider the following questions while you sit in your daily meditation:

- Have you drunk pure water that fills your mind with light?

- Have you breathed the breath that creates you?

- Have you moved to the earth's heartbeat?

- Have you swum with water, filling her with all your mysteries?

- Have you risen from the ashes to find that your pure essence has been refined?

- Have you found yourself broken, only to see you have become stronger?

We find ourselves lost in the middle of the ocean, or at least that's what we are told, only to find the ocean's heart beneath our soul. We come closer to see our many reflections. This is the place where we began. We rest and wait to be taken by her loving hand. In this dream, I awake to see what I am. The Sea Goddess says, "You are important to me, for you hold my heart in your hands."

Common Questions for a Sea Priestess

Am I afraid of success? Is that why I come up short every time?

Start listing all those times you have not "come up short," and that will cause you to focus on success.

How do I deal with fear holding me back?

Call it what it is, an untruth teller!

Exercise #1

Write one thing you want to accomplish, just one thing. Write one step you will do today to bring you closer to your dream. Then record the results of that one step. Take one step each day, until you cross the finish line.

Exercise #2

Make a "Vision Board"

Obtain a big sheet of paper and write the following on it:

This is now my life! I create my life; I live my life this way.

Then place one dream on this sheet of paper—draw it or cut pictures out of a magazine. Make this sheet of paper very appealing to you. As you develop this Vision

Board, write all the excuses you have to cause your dream not to become accomplished. Then, as time goes by, deal with each of these dream robbers. This is your life. Instead of removing your dreams, remove the excuses. To be a finisher, one must first begin.

↢ 8 ↣

Fly!

He who takes his teachings and applies them increases his knowledge.

—Hawaiian proverb

We are told, with no direct words, that our purpose is somehow withheld from us by something bigger than us. So for decades, we wonder what our purpose is. Why will Deity not reveal what I am to be? We wait to hear directions for our own life from something outside ourselves. We are informed to wait, so we wait. We are told our lives are certainly not in our hands and neither is understanding.

Many generations have lived under those life-killing beliefs that serve no one. Two things were taken from us; two gifts given, then hidden from us: free will and our purposes. We are fully capable of having many missions, not just one.

Some individuals do not like the idea that they need to find out for themselves what free will means and how it is related to them. We were never told why free will is important or its full meaning! Some individuals will understand this precept, while others will not want to know, and that's okay. We all remember in our own time and in our own way. The objective of this lesson is to place a seed of hope within your heart, to show how utterly important we are to the whole of creation and the grand scheme of things and to reclaim our identity.

No one really knows when it all started or why; yet ever so quietly, and with a smile on their faces, "they" came to take something away from us. We knew something was missing, but were taught distraction and self-doubt to keep us busy so that we would not focus on what was seemingly missing within us. No one knows who started this removal, but the first disconnect probably happened at the beginning of space and time as we know it.

In no direct words, we are still told every day that we need permission to be what we already are. We are told without words, "It is not up to you; you have no control over yourself, over your own will." To compensate for our missing parts, we have spent eons requesting or craving validation from the very ones who have removed our free will. Though approval from others is sweet, it never begins to bring back our light, our rights, or our purposes.

It is *we* who choose our purpose! When we were born, each of us selected this so-called time and space. Each of us selected which mother we were birthed through and, for some, our father. We selected how and what we were going to learn in this time and space before we popped onto the scene. It is we who chose our purpose and plan, both here and on the other side.

I feel compelled to say this again: I do not care if a famous or very ancient person said something to create a philosophy; that does not make it an absolute truth.

Focus on your own ideals and purposes. I do know who does have the answers for your life—it is you. I do know who knows your purposes—it is you. We must say no to some famous quotes that cause us to do little or nothing. These life-limiting quotes need to be removed from our thought process.

Two rights were quietly hidden from us and will be reclaimed by only us! No one can do it for us; it is our responsibility to wake up, take back free will, and begin to remember why we needed it in the first place. We have forgotten that we are sovereign, and because we are sovereign, we decide our purpose; thus expansion and evolution continue their path through us. That is what "it" is all about: consciousness growth and free-will expansion.

We were separated from our free will and now we come to regain what was, is, and always will be rightfully ours to utilize. We will find our vitality, our self, our family of consciousness and thrive again. Doing so will reveal new levels of perception, deeper insights, our Sea Priestess identity, our strength, our beauty, and our inexhaustible glory. By utilizing our free will, we will trust ourselves once again, trust our own decisions again, and trust our own life and purposes again.

We are all here for a reason: to learn what free will is and how to use this right as a Sea Priestess. By utilizing free will as a Sea Priestess, we add to the Universe. Sea Priestesses always give to a situation, person, place, thing, or event—never subtracting, only adding. Trust your free will.

Stop thinking about the incorrect definition given to us and ask Deity to give and show you the real meaning of free will. We are about to take flight here, my beautiful Sea Priestess. Allow all those beings sent to be our companions to surround us and show us our wings. The Source gives us free will's real definition and its nature. The more we understand what free will is and its nature, the more free will blossoms within our lives. The more it blossoms, the more we will use it. The more we use it, the more we will become free, and freedom will be returned with all its benefits.

Free will was given to us for a real reason, an important reason. Begin this exciting exploration by seeing yourself flying high so that you can see the vast horizon, our horizon, your horizon. This right was lovingly given so that you may fly to heights that only you can reach. Now see yourself flying. See yourself flying to a distant place where you are going to capture what was taken from you so long ago.

Do not be concerned; you will not be alone. You will see other souls flying to the same place to recapture their lost free will. Enjoy your flight! Do not forget to keep your focus strong. Fear not, for free will is rightfully yours to possess and use, to know, to develop, and to fly home. Experience this free will and its purpose! Our consciousness has a thousand wings flying in every direction; we swim through the cosmos while all our parts take the flight called free will. We freely willed to be here and to take part in this beautiful dream. We chose to freely fly through all of this expansion through the wind and through the waters.

Flying Resources

Meditation #1

In your meditation, as you fly off into the blue sky, sing:

Flying high in the big blue sky.
I reclaim my right I sing.
For I will learn what free will means!
I now know I am free.
Fly, fly, flying high I sing!
I hear and reclaim my song within.

Now contemplate the following prompts to allow you to open to free will.

- Fill your cup first with song, so that you may give from your freedom.
- You are in many places and many dimensions.
- You are many beings.
- You are within many times and spaces.
- I come from the future and the past to stand in this moment with you, O lovely Sea Priestess. The more you learn about you, the more you will learn about me. Am I in you? Or are you in me? I gently rock you from your sleep. Do you feel me rocking you?
- You are loved beyond measure.
- You were always there and here with me.
- Your soul has always burned as it flies farther and farther, closer and closer.
- Your answers are close by and within you.
- Trust yourself to be the world's hope for all that is.

No one can take your free will; it was always here within you. Your free will is designed to help you know what you want, not someone outside you telling or influencing your perceptions. Free will is your backbone saying, "I will not move until I decide and measure all the facts for myself. I will decide to freely use my own will to manifest in my life." Free will says there was no cost for this right to be given to us. It takes strength to wield free will's forces.

Common Questions for a Sea Priestess

I do not know what my purpose is!

> Yes, you do. Why do you think you have so many guides, totems, ancestors, many types of energies in many frequencies, on many levels, in many dimensions? The list goes on and on—all to be utilized by and for you! The Universes communicate with you every day, even this one.

How do I reclaim something I supposedly already have?

> A right cannot be utilized if the right has never been used or taught. Ask yourself how many times in the past year you made a fully aware, free-will decision. Ask yourself how many times you have lived in this right of free will. How many times have you used free will as a tool to gain your purpose?

Is free will just deciding what religion or tradition to follow?

> Free will is much bigger than deciding what tradition or religion to follow. Free will has little to do with making a decision or which dogma to follow. In fact, it has nothing to do with following anything or anyone. This most magnificent right is designed to

be used as a tool for our evolution, our freedom, our blessings; it is our free will, given to us freely to use freely for our life!

How will exploring my free will help me?

Free will is like talking about love. Everyone thinks they know what it is and everyone has at least a surface definition taught to them. Everyone thinks they know all of love's benefits and how love draws good things into one's life. Go deeper, my friend. Just because a definition is in the dictionary does not make it complete or correct. Just because we read about love does not mean we know about love.

Like love, free will must be experienced before you can see its benefits and lessons. Just for fun, give yourself the goal that for one year you will explore the notion of free will; you will be profoundly changed in that time. The same is true for love. Utilize love as if it were a healing agent. Approach love as if you were learning for the first time about love directly from Source and apply this divine love to your life.

Exercise #1

Thirty-Day Meditation

Meditate for five minutes per day for thirty days. Ask the High Priestess of the Sea Priestess Temple to come to you within a dream or meditation and show you where to go. Just rest and be still, listening for her waters to flow through you once more.

Using your favorite meditation method, rest in a peaceful repose and allow the Sea Priestess Queen to speak to you. Allow yourself to trust what you hear. Listen with your entire body of water, allowing yourself to see other dimensions, other perceptions, other definitions of what is. Listen with all your highly tuned senses—listen. The answers will deepen as the thirty days pass. Feel yourself going deeper and deeper into the water. You will be given the exact measure you give to the inquiry; enjoy this process!

You will experience your first initiation by saying and agreeing with the statements in the covenant at the back of this book. The second initiation will take place spontaneously in one of your dreams; pure love is poured upon your soul, and you will know when you awaken you have been changed and awakened to selflessly help others for the rest of your life.

The ocean breezes now begin to breathe within the ebb and flow of your watery lungs. Sense the salt air surround you, sense the saltwater inside you! Fly, baby, fly through the waters of the Universes; this is your domain! Sense what belongs to you!

Exercise #2

Ocean Mother

Read the following quote before you go to sleep tonight:

> *Source of All Earth's Life.*
> *Ever-changing cradle of creation*
> *You are, She who dances with the Moon.*
> *Each wave celebrates Your power and fierce beauty.*
> *The silence of the shore speaks the wisdom of the ages.*
> *May the waves fill us with Your sacred wisdom.*
> *Your names flow from our tongues in reverence.*
> —author unknown

9

Divination

Whether you think you can or think you can't, either way you are right.

—Henry Ford

Divination Attuning

Individuals desire to find out what will be as if their future has already been written, desiring to know what will come so that they may use the information to walk in wisdom. There are differing schools of thought on predestination. The Correllian Tradition believes in both predetermined destiny and that we decide our destiny. When individuals ask to have a reading, the main underlying reason is, "Will everything be okay?" or "Will my family be okay?"

Others want to have outside validation or confirmation of what they have already done or have already decided to do, asking, "Is this the right decision?" Of course, some individuals want to know if they are going to meet someone special or if they are coming into money; both serious questions for the seeker. Everyone needs wise counsel from water's living springs. Wise spiritual counsel through divination and dreams is like a mother lovingly embracing her child and saying, "I am here, with you always."

Divination confirms that we are being dreamt by a dreamer, as we, too, dream our creations into existence. We are a dream that dreams day and night. We are the "purpose" of a dreamer that dreams us, which lives within "its" dream; we are the promise. We were made on purpose for a purpose. How magnificent, how lovely, how powerful that we are a mutable, ever-expanding dream. Because of this, our possibilities are endless; the world's possibilities are endless.

Within this dream, we are able to travel by many meridian types, the matrix, our very core to find what we need to see for the so-called future. What does divination or dreams have to do with water? Divination, water, and dreams are clear looking glasses to every "moment" that is found here in this ever-present dream. We cannot study water or dreams for very long before seeing the so-called "future" clearly, and we can then begin to utilize our inner senses. As we look into our very own reflecting pool, there is no denying our "future," because there it is staring right back at us. Goddess/God desires that you know everything you desire to know; for those who want to avail themselves of divination skills, knowing them is a sacred skill that carries much responsibility and diplomacy. Wisdom is found in water dreams, as both lie in your hands.

Seeing What the Water Sees

Water is mentioned in almost every culture, within a vast array of myths and traditions, when discussing dreams, divination, and prophecy. Nostradamus (1503–1566), renowned as France's greatest visionary, used water for divination.

One of Nostradamus's prophecies, which has not yet been fulfilled, is the Hall of Records prophecy, which explains that wisdom shall be found in an "Urn." In ancient times, it was the urn that would hold water, and it was the urn that would be used as a measuring device. In Rigveda 10.125, it says: "My origin is in the waters, in the ocean."

The Hall of Records Prophecy

> They will come to discover the hidden topography of the land [at Giza]. The urns holding wisdom within the monuments [the Pyramids] opened up, their contents will cause the understanding of holy philosophy to expand greatly, white exchanged for black, falsehoods exposed, new wisdom replacing the established traditions that no longer work.

I find it curious that this wisdom will be found in a water jug! How appropriate! In the Vedas, we read that water holds wisdom. That is, the Mesopotamian water god Ea, full of wisdom, dispenses counsel to the gods. The wisdom of water gods was the main function of their age. In the Hellenic world, the wisest were referred to as the "old men of the sea."

Another association to water wisdom and consciousness is the very ancient Lake Manasarovar, which resides high in the gorgeous Tibetan mountains. Many believe this area is the very center of the world. Millions travel every year to this lake to receive direction, wisdom, and healing from the waters, visiting the lake then going home to dream for divination and enlightenment. The meaning of the word Manasarovar is "Lake of Consciousness and Enlightenment." We are and live in a moving, living-energy ocean of consciousness that quickens everything.

Hermes Trismegistus's riddle also supports the notion that wisdom is found in water. According to Shah and many other insightful writers, Hermes inscribed on the Emerald Tablet this riddle or "key" that represents the inner principles of alchemy, the Great Work. The following is Shah's rendering of the Emerald Tablet quote; it is my opinion that it describes water, how it functions, and the part it plays within every wonder through wisdom that is to return hope to the world once again.

The Emerald Tablet

> The truth, certainly truest, without untruth.
>
> What is above is like what is below.
>
> What is below is what is above.
>
> The miracle of unity is to be attained.
>
> Everything is formed from the contemplation of unity, and all things come from unity, by means of adaptation.
>
> Its parents are the Sun and the Moon.
>
> It was borne by the wind and nurtured by the Earth.
>
> Every wonder is from it, and its power is complete.
>
> Throw it upon earth, and earth will separate from fire.
>
> The impalpable separated from the palpable.
>
> Through wisdom it rises slowly from the world to heaven.

Then it descends to the world, combining the power of the upper and the lower.

Thus you shall have the illumination of the world, and darkness will disappear.

This is the power of all strength. It overcomes that which is delicate and penetrates through solids.

This was the means of the creation of the world.

And in the future wonderful developments will be made, and this is the way.

I am Hermes the Threefold Sage, so named because I hold the three elements of all the Wisdom.

I believe that if you replace the word "it" with the word "water" in Hermes's riddle, you can unveil the truth about the wisdom of water and the keys it holds.

Divination Suggestions

All divination mediums work in the same general way, as you would divine with a crystal ball. Going into an alpha, or dream, state, you must enter stillness, then dream to see what you shall see. The following is just a small sample of water divination. Ask your ancestors for guidance. Do not depend on them; completely depend on your past experiences and knowledge. Think of the ancestors as your partners.

To start, first pick your form of divination. You may choose any of the following options. Gaze into:

- any body of water on the full moon,
- a large dark bowl of water,

- a blackened mystic mirror (mirrors represent water), or
- a mirror with a candle at night or in a dark room.

You may also choose to listen instead of using your sight, in which case you can listen to a lake, pond, well, spring, or any other body of water. When listening to water, do not be hypnotized; stay focused and actively listen to the answer to your question. The sound of water also heals.

During your divination, whether by sight or hearing, feel the water, either with your entire body or just a hand or foot. Allow water wisdom to come through touch, through your skin. The water ancients and World Walkers listen for or sense wisdom through their skin.

You can also call in dolphin divination. By simply "seeing" a dolphin, finish your thought by thinking of what you are dreaming for your immediate future. In other words, begin a sentence and allow dolphin divination to complete the statement.

Next, stir water and see what you shall see. You may see waves appear on the surface. Waves travel in threes, which are called a "wave train." The last wave of the wave train is the most powerful for reading and receiving wisdom. Reading the wave means interpreting the wave. Waves reveal the many environments we create by our consciousness. Another way to say this is that we all create many stories and conditions within each story line. Essentially each wave is a new creation; just like us, each wave produces knowledge. We receive this knowledge through our Higher Self or inner senses. Through meditation, Deity causes us to become aware of our Higher Self and our capacity to understand what nature is teaching us; this includes the wave.

When talking about water and the sea, one needs to stress that the sea holds the same substance as many lands and animals: salt. Salt has much wisdom locked in every grain. The alchemists say, "Whoever knows the salt knows the secret of the ancient sages." Salt is also a symbol of the soul and the worlds it lives in.

Salt represents the earth element, which is a firm foundation and a vessel that holds all water on earth. The wisdom of salt is revealed when we allow ourselves to actively become aware of what is being presented. Salt is a living consciousness and is trying to evolve just like us. Salt as an energetic element that helps free all the outworn assumptions that hinder us from piercing our self-made stories or reality system. Salt also reminds us that all our knowledge and purposes are available to us, thus enriching our reality production. You have set up your challenges, and you have also set up the varied approaches to solving every one of them.

You can even use a single water drop to read. Simply dip a finger into water and allow a single drop of water to land on a flat surface in a well-lit room or outside on a bright day. We read the single drop of water just like we would read a crystal ball—through intuition. We study the shapes inside the drop of water to see if the shape resembles something. If the shapes seem to be in the distance, the event will happen in the far future. If the shape seems close to the surface, the event will happen soon. If the reflected light is multicolored, this represents that whatever you are creating will be a success. If no colors are coming through, you are in a rest mode in your life, working yet not stretching your creativity. If there are dark shadows within the drop of water, this is telling you to go inward and consider everything in your life—essentially, a time of involution.

Additionally, you can hold a shell close to your ear and, while in an alpha or dream meditation state, you will hear a story of old or it will tell your story. Shell divinations always begin their muttering the same way, by saying, "Let us start a story, let us continue the dream."

All divination and dreams are not for entertainment or for building the overdeveloped ego, but for quiet soul growth.

You can listen to the voices of the waters and winds; you are able to receive and give. Both are equally important, giving and receiving.

Ahoy

In meditation, begin to start your treasure hunt; a great place to start is to examine all your "belief/thought systems," one by one. I recommend tackling one belief/thought system per month.

Once you have identified a belief system you would like to work on, ask yourself the following questions:

1. Has this belief/thought system helped or hindered me in the past?

2. Does this thought move me forward?

3. Does this thought change me?

4. Does this thought fully express who I am?

5. Does this thought make me feel good? If it does not, consider removing it from your life.

Emotional thoughts are one of the main non-word languages Goddess/God uses to speak directly to us, no middle man needed. Goddess/God makes things crystal clear to you through your emotions/thoughts. Decide to live in good emotions, one day at a time—for some, one second at a time—and watch what happens. Ask yourself, "What do I feel today?" Is it good or bad? If it is good, Goddess/God is saying to you, "Good! Keep doing what you are doing!" If you feel bad, Goddess/God is saying, "Knock it off! Stop doing what you are doing, and rethink what you are doing on a consistent basis."

Building Your Water Astral Temple

With strong emotion, feeling (no words), begin the process of making one of your astral temples; build it anyplace on the astral plane—using emotion! Feel it into existence. If you have difficulties with stirring up emotion, dive deep within your astral body. For some, astral travel takes great effort and time to learn, while others instinctively know how to consciously journey. While there are many ways to astral travel, these are the steps for a Sea Priestess.

1. Find a comfortable, quiet place to sit or lie down.

2. Enter stillness. (You can follow Meditation #1 at the end of this chapter for more help entering stillness.) Be still for five minutes and allow your mind to become hyperaware of what is going on around you, of your breathing, and of the sounds around you. When thoughts of the day drift in, just allow them to drift out again.

3. Continue relaxing as you focus on your rhythmic breathing; think about the rhythmic sound and movement of the small waves that touch the shoreline and match the wave's motion to the rhythm of your breath.

4. Breathe in rhythm with the waves for several minutes.

5. Invoke your Deity in whatever form feels right to you. We Sea Priestesses call upon our beloved ancestors and the spirit of water to be with us and guide us on this journey.

6. Now see yourself being engulfed in pure, glimmering, silver-white light. This is an interstellar spaceship of sorts that holds your consciousness; though, in reality, it is your consciousness that holds everything. Feel this light swirling all around you. Feel it begin to lift you slowly upward. The engine of this radiant silver-white vessel is your open mind. Your mind takes you everywhere through water.

7. Now allow yourself to first see the ceiling of the room you are in, then see yourself moving past the ceiling.

8. Tell your vessel through your open mind to take you high in the air for a few minutes, if this is your first time, or fly through your neighborhood. When you feel comfortable, try flying to the highest mountain on earth or to another country or even another time. Take short trips in the beginning. Even if the trip is only three seconds, you are strengthening

your ability for astral travel. Then when you feel you are ready to travel to the ocean floor, follow the rest of the instructions here.

9. (Note: If you have been taught and believe that negative entities can harm you while on the astral plane, then if you encounter a being you perceive as negative, you should fly high and keep flying high until you can look back and see that the seemingly negative presence is gone. Remember, as humans nothing in the astral plane can harm us because it is we who designed this reality plane to create our physical plane. There is much to discuss about astral travel, yet this is a great start for you to begin today.)

10. Once you have reached the bottom of the ocean, lie on its floor, feeling her emotions. Once again, do not think—only feel. Request Goddess to help you; then allow her to show you how to feel deeply. Goddess will not tell you how to build your temple; that is your responsibility. Your temple will never be complete, because it always changes. While building your water temple, the temple will communicate with you. Just like anything you build in the physical plane, its full purpose is revealed in the midst of action, in the midst of building. When it is time to return to your physical plane, thank Deity, the spirit of water, and your ancestors for their protection and aid. See yourself still inside the glimmering, silver-white light vessel, gently returning you to the place where you began your journey.

Divination Resources

Meditation #1

Stillness Enters

Speak the following words as you enter your meditation:

> I lay my mind aside so that I may connect to the cosmic mind and the Higher Self.
>
> I choose to remember what was always mine but have forgotten through time.
>
> I return to my soul's core, returning to my sovereign free will, to relearn where and why I am.
>
> I was created when Deity was created, and Deity has no beginning.
>
> How may one return to the soul when we are already here?
>
> I fall deep inside creation's cauldron, with quantum love who created my soul.
>
> I fall into my collective soul, seeing how immense I am.
>
> Deep space is shallow compared to this cauldron, this ever-expanding soul.

Go into stillness, open your eyes, and gently gaze, seeing yourself sitting in a huge cauldron of water—your tub! Just relax and see what you will see, using your skin as eyes and ears. Meditation is about tuning in, not tuning out. Focus on entering your peace. Expect the unexpected. If preconceived ideas are formed, that is all you will receive. Meditation is about receiving new information through old ways. Do not think, just be.

Because we live in a society that believes results are supposed to happen instantly, we can be disappointed when nothing or very little happens at the beginning of an exercise or task. It takes time, and that is a good thing. This exercise will help your consciousness to expand and show itself to you, a little at a time. Be patient and kind to yourself. Results/answers may come months or even years later. There are times when nothing happens for months; then all of a sudden, a flood of information comes. How perfect! Move past your trained "thinker," move into your emotions and will, free.

Water activates everything. While in your meditation, consider these lessons:

- Uncover hidden treasures that were buried long ago—with your help. Do not give away the best parts of you; do not give up your power to be what you were designed to be from the beginning. There is no need.

- Delve into deep waters to regain your treasures, taking back what is rightfully yours. Reclaim your full emotions so that you may fully operate your manifestation mechanism and may clearly see again.

- Working with divination and dreams is digging for buried treasure that has your name on it. Why do you think so many hearts leap a little when the words "buried treasure" are uttered? Deeply imprinted within our DNA, collectively, we all know the truth: there are buried treasures, and they all belong to us, treasures worth more than mere money. Buried in the sands of time, and under the sea, these tools are yours to reclaim and utilize; they are gifts that are living tools. If you are not going to use your tools/gifts, then rebury them until you are ready to take on the responsibility and free will to do the shadow work.

- Do you know there is a treasure, indeed a promise, that lives within you? *Are you ready to approach the Holy of Holies?* Strong, controlled emotion is the beginning of seeing that a tree is more than its color, shape, and height; that a bird is more than what we see with our physical eyes. We are beginning to experience our song, our love, our sixth sense. We can regain what we lost long ago. We are returning to our roots.

- We already live in pure love; we already stand together in her wise, bright light.

Common Questions for a Sea Priestess

Why is studying water so important?

Everything can be studied as a single subject. I chose water, because "it" has chosen me.

Why is divination important?

The ability to interpret, comprehend, and attune with the cosmic mind is more than seeing if you are going to win the lottery. Divining dreams is a natural skill to see other dimensions, uncovering old and new truths. Let the unlearning begin so that all our false conceptions and preconceptions are washed away.

Exercise #1

For six months or longer, experiment with a few of the water-divination methods discussed in this chapter.

Exercise #2

The Water Web is a massive, interconnecting web formed by water moving in every direction. Its size is immeasurable and extends to everywhere we know. The Water Web can be entered through any cloud, and it resides in both the physical and the astral worlds. The Water Web is a multipathway to heighten communications between all Sea Priestesses and a depository to hold water wisdom. Sea Priestesses are guardians of the Water Web.

Impressions through Expression

The entirety of water divination contains millions of paths. You are a path. Begin to feel yourself becoming a source of water. Anytime you pass a river, creek, pond—any pool of water—look into it and see yourself, then see your Higher Self. Say in your own words, "I know I am this pool of water. I know it knows, and I love it!" Go back to this pool of water as often as you can. Watch your changes, and watch how the water changes! Begin to see yourself as a moving stream of water; watch yourself traveling down in many directions at once. Visit this pool of water in your dreams; be the stream in your waking hours.

These are both important aspects, because this exercise allows you to be more than just skin and bones, more than one personality, more than the physical realm. This exercise gradually allows you to move away from the physical realm, redefining yourself. This exercise also helps you to see your dreams during the day and helps you develop your astral body for the advanced work of the World Walkers.

◈ 10 ◈

Who Is a Sea Priestess?

First, unless you know yourself, all knowing is useless.
—Taoist saying

One of the saddest concepts that ever entered into any culture is when an individual or group that you do not know, nor have ever met, gleefully hands over a measuring stick, saying this is your standard and this is what you shall attain. So from that day forward, everything we do, say, have, or look like is measured by that standard outside us.

I hope that you can see through this controlling ploy that sets people up to be good little consumers; however, this standard stick has gone deeper into some individuals' minds, and they spend most of their lives within this competitive concept. Or there are people who think that they know how you should behave without ever finding out about your culture, your sensibilities, or your illnesses, if that applies. I am not talking about fashion trends but how one lives, your choices on how you want to live your life. No one should feel pressured into wearing something unless one is in the military services, the priesthood, or at a school that has a dress code.

From this day forward, it will be you who defines your world, your definition of perfection, and your perception of freely living under your own design. Focusing on your story, not stories made up by others, start living your story! One can learn much from other stories of old; conversely, you will learn more by learning your own story. The best story ever told and experienced will be yours! Your story and life are second to none.

Perfection is in the being; perfection is being completely what you are. Like the brown maple leaf that falls to the ground, that is perfection. We live in stages, and each life has its own lessons, perfection, and worth. The child is willing and open to all the wonders of the world; the teen has no fear; the young adult has abounding energy, trying to learn everything all at once and having fun exploring all the possibilities surrounding her.

Middle age brings focus and well-seasoned accomplishments and the realization that we do not know everything, which brings in more knowledge. Younger seniors usher in contentment, compassion, teaching, and wisdom; yet there is a caveat here—this occurs only if they were willing to learn with a nonjudgmental mind throughout their life.

The elderly fondly remember their past now that time has softened the harsh blows of life; they see that, by living and learning, they have grown and can see the finish line. Peace enters as they ready themselves to return to their other home in Spirit.

As a youth, while all my friends would be talking to other children or teens, I would sneak into a bar or go into a church or go to a park bench, hoping I could hear the stories of a friendly elderly person. As a young adult, I worked in a nursing home in Woodbury, New Jersey, for the same reason. Even though their stories had different verbiage, and they talked of another time, I saw through all of that and paid attention to the very essence of the Goddess that would pour out of them quite easily along with their words of wisdom. My definition of perfection is birth and death and everything in the middle—all beautiful.

Life is the soul's wonderful, colorful adventure, learning and collecting information like berries in a basket to bring back home to share with the family. The soul is here to experience life so that Goddess/God may enjoy being united as well. This reality system is not our home; we just visit here for short periods of the human-made construct called time, which is perfect. Everything is excellent, whether or not there are skills employed. Being accurate depends on which standard is being utilized, whose truth or perception is in play.

Perfection is also water and nature, and, of course, we are part of both—there is no distinction. Water never diminishes and nothing can stop it. The same is true of us. Water is forever changing and is forever. The same is true for us. It may become part of a puddle, then rise as vapor to the sky to become part of a cloud, only to fall again as a snowflake or rain, entering a lake or reservoir that is purified so that a person may drink the water.

As water enters a body, it lives and reacts with all the beauty and minds that reside within. Scientists have even said that each nation of germs that lives within us acts as one mind; our immune system is smarter than we think, setting up barriers and movement for our protection. Once water arrives within our bodies, it acts as a recorder, collecting information as well as disseminating information to every part of our being. The piece of information can just be saying hello, acknowledging us while regenerating, cleansing, healing, helping release old constructs, and so on. Once expelled from the body, like an offering on a living altar, it returns to a lake or puddle once again—always on the move as it is changing.

We are the same way. We are always moving, ever changing, on both the inside and the outside; nothing can come between us and our Source. Nothing can stop us from our journey. Water is the only thing that can go through stone, and, spiritually, so can we. Not even our shadows can stop us; all of our shadows have always been created and kept alive by none other than us!

As consciousness and part of Source, we created everything. We are bigger than anything we have created, especially our own shadows and walls. Once you have earnestly fully experienced life on your terms and proclaim power over your shadows, then you will feel a new sense bubbling up within you, a new day dawning, a new way to enter your life fully, a new strength that will be filled with confidence and assured footing. Not arrogance or a big ego but a strong knowing that you have walked through choppy, dark waters to know your answer, your hope, your happiness, your wisdom.

All you needed has always been waiting for you—your way, your time. The ability to change this reality system is inside your perfect hands. Every single person has chosen to be here, at this time, to do their part for this age. That is how important you are to this system. That is how much you are needed. That is how much you are loved by the Goddess/God. That is how ancient you are! That is how perfect you are! Not worldly perfection but Divine perfection by quantum love.

Now that you have worked with your shadows, destroying some and diminishing others, you are ready to learn about your water, your story, your many purposes. Now that you have completed this course, you are ready to enter the waters to learn and to move within the waters of a Sea Priestess. It is time to claim and take care of a body of water or more than one body; it is up to you. You will find me next to Hiva's sunken temple in the South Pacific waters. I will send my song as you send yours, across the sea to enter your water. We are glad we have found you again. This is the beginning of becoming a Sea Priestess or Priest. The lessons are learned through your life, your waters, and every animal that lives under, above, or beside the water—that includes you.

Though not mandatory, some Sea Priestesses make it their business to help support water causes, while others are shamans, high priestesses of a beautiful tradition, healers, teachers, World Walkers, farmers, gardeners, or oceanographers who work near or on bodies of water. Only those of pure heart and motives can enter and remain within the water.

Sometimes, it is more reflective to study what a species cannot accomplish, though Correllian thought always stresses that we explain everything in positive terms instead of what it is not. A person with great arrogance is not a Sea Priestess. Nobody is attracted to a person who thinks they know more than anyone else; ultimately, they do not know more than anyone.

If a person is tearing down another group or person, this shows that she/he has fallen into judgment. Of course everyone has a bad day, but this person always talks negatively about other people. The reason why they would not make a good Sea Priestess is because their hands are already full, thus there is no or little time to take care of the Great Work or take care of water. Day after day judging, judging; and judging will tear you down, not them. This kind of negative behavior will render you helpless, not them.

A well-meaning person who appears to know everything knows nothing of us. Only the humble seeker may enter our watery realm. Yes, there are times to rise up and handle a situation if someone is trying to interfere with your dream, family, or friends; identify what they are trying to do to the group and handle this issue in a wise way. Yes, there are times to remove such personalities from your life so that your dream returns to your vision, not theirs. Sometime we need to do a difficult thing to clear our path to our dream and vision, but always do it with compassion. A Sea Priestess is many good things.

The World Walkers' Water Web Introduction

In 2000, the International Hydrographic Organization established the Southern ocean and determined its boundaries; thus the world now has five oceans—the Indian, Atlantic, Arctic, Pacific, and now the Southern ocean, creating a connected web—a web that until this day has been waiting for us to unveil its mysteries. It is the largest living organism on this planet, moving and responding to the rhythm of the cosmos, giving protection and sustaining every life form. I believe the moon controls water, while water controls every living thing. Every "body" of water is part of the Water Web, not just in this world but across all Universes.

Water records information from the entire Universe, then distributes information for all who are willing to attune to water and receive its ancient wisdom. As a wise communicator, water records, watches, and serves as a master guide, communicating her cosmic history and how to expand human consciousness. Communicating how everything exists in this one moment, as different worlds unfold, water makes it clear there is no division. Water is a master guide that is generous when assigning spirit guides to all who enter the living sea, fully prepared to give all it has to all it touches.

If a soul needs two thousand guides, then so be it! If a soul needs only a few guides, then so be it. Every minute dictates how many guides you need to be able to change, move, grow, and evolve. Some guides are a little pushy, but you are the one who has the final say; others lift you, while building you sand castles on the beach and throwing shells at your feet. Water is also protective, leading you through choppy waters, leading you to deep, still waters, deep ocean earth caves—all slowly built by water, slowly molding stones by flowing around and through them until space is made. I always like to say, there are more possibilities in nothing than in something.

Again, seemingly in a different moment, a different world appears in the Universe's teaching, another life perspective. When you gaze upon a stream or puddle, water will resonate with you.

You are already plugged into the universal Water Web; you are already there—or, more correctly stated, you are already here. You already know about it through your ancient imaginations and dreams; imagination is the gateway to the Water Web. Imagination is the engine that transports us here. As Albert Einstein once said, "Imagination is more important than knowledge."

The Water Web is a loving, mystical web woven by billions of moving streams, moving in every conceivable and inconceivable direction. First, there are small streams—created by rain, sleet, snow, and hail—that all sink deep within the earth's crust until they reach the inner Mother Ocean, living far below the earth's surface. It takes one generation for this stream to return to the earth's surface again, touching Mother before returning to us as drinking water.

Second, there are large streams that flow horizontally, staying mostly on the surface—all oceans, seas, rivers, and lakes.

The third stream set consists of large and very defined rivers that flow vertically upward, toward the sky, usually starting at the equator. Some of these vertical rivers span 480 miles wide and flow a distance of 4,800 miles upward. Some streams are defined and constant, while others change shape and speed.

The fourth set of Universal streams comes from space, in a vertical fashion. First the water enters as ice, then as cosmic rain. The fifth set of currents is floating streams, which move in every direction; they are mist, fog, and clouds. The sixth stream set is the vast, incomprehensible ocean that all planets live within. Some planets float or rest on this thin mist of space fabric, others are resting at the bottom, while others are suspended in the cosmic sea.

The seventh spring is the living Source that lives within us all. Our streams flow in every direction and relate to every other stream. We are part of the Water Web—we are a small part, we are a large part, we are the Web in its completeness, the Universe is the Web in its completeness, with us at the center. We, too, flow as deep as the downward streams on and within the earth, as wide and high as the vertical streams. Rivers flow down, diagonally, and up. Every stream thread weaving, intersecting, moving over and under, forward and backward, creating an intricate, magnificent, ever-changing Water Web.

Connecting to the Water Web

How can a person become connected to the Water Web?

How much "shadow work" one does is in exact proportion to how much one may "use" the Web. But remember that you are already part of the Web. Knowing thyself is the beginning and end of everything. We come from space on a water drop, then return in a cosmic flow, excited to return to our starry home. We come back again and again, weaving our part of the Water Web.

Another way to look at the Water Web is that it is a colossal stream of chakras that run through and around the entire single "One," including all Universes within and without. There are more than seven main chakras. One chakra consists of millions of chakras, just like us. Like everything, you are just relearning a skill that you already know; you are remembering how to experience and utilize something that has always been yours from the beginning.

Entering the Water Web

This is one of many ways to work with the Water Web.

1. To become more aware of your connection to the Water Web, look up at the clouds and, in the beginning, select the smallest, wispiest, unformed cloud you can find.

2. While gazing at your very tiny, wispy cloud, think "dissolve, dissolve, dissolve . . ." until it does. Warning: Do not think "move," because that is what the wispy cloud will do.

3. You have now opened the Water Web gate; be blessed. Enter the Water Web that connects every water type on this planet as well as on the farthest star. Decide if you want to close your eyes or keep them open. Decide if you are to sit, lie down, or stand.

4. Think in your mind only using pictures from this point forward. Instead of saying to yourself, "I will sit at this sacred gate and linger for a while," see yourself doing it. Open your imagination!

5. If it is difficult to stop the thinker, then allow the disruptive thoughts to just float by, giving them no energy. After meditating for a season, it will become much easier to enter into stillness where there is no thinking, only seeing, hearing, touching, smelling, and sensing with your third eye.

6. Once in a while, have someone watch you from a distance, taking notice of all the wonderful things that sometimes happen in your vicinity.

7. Now that you are inside the World Walker's Water Web, you are now ready to receive or send information. Send or receive healing in every form. Send or receive change in every form. Give or receive teachings. In time, this is where you will visit many astral healing centers.

8. For now, just enjoy feeling all the wonderful energies. Explore each living stream by entering this

meditation on a semi-daily basis. If you do not enjoy meditation, then come here in your dreams.

9. Once you feel you are ready to work within the Streams, put on your Water Web swimsuit and swim! After all, this is our purpose, as World Walkers—to serve, explore, teach, and be catalysts for birthing; for evolution, becoming Thetan, and returning to what we were. This Web is one way of many ways: the Water Way.

Some may just enjoy lingering at the gate for now, and that is okay, because the more souls at the gate, the more energy is instilled into the Web—everyone does their part.

Moving in the Water Web

Use the exercise above to move into the Water Web at least once a week, more if you choose. This exercise will help develop communication skills with the Water Web. All the living streams and water guides will teach how to receive massive amounts of information so that you, in turn, may pass it along the same way. Water guides will teach you to access all water worlds; the Water Web is one such technique that leads to many water paths.

More "others" will reveal themselves to you as you show them how to walk the Rainbow Cloud. The Rainbow Cloud is the ring around the moon at night, sometimes called a moonbow. This is our circle; all Sea Priestesses can look up to the moon and know we are seeing and living under the same moon, the same Rainbow Cloud. Many Sea Priestesses do not live by the sea, so this Rainbow Cloud around the moon ensures us that we are together and trying to learn about our realities. Be strong, for we are Water Walkers.

Coming Out of the Water Web Meridian

When you are finished enjoying the Water Web, see yourself coming out of the gate, then back into your body—the body in this time and space, on this plane. See the gate close behind you as you come back; see the wispy cloud come back.

Most people do not cause the wispy little cloud to come back, which is perfectly fine; in time you will, if that is your desire. Some take a quick astral trip to the nearest body of water for a cleansing dip, even though this is not necessary to do.

After touchdown, ground and release.

(NOTE: If you want to try dissolving bigger clouds to access bigger gates, go for it. Every cloud is, in fact, a completely different gate to explore; all memory is located here. This is not about dissolving clouds; the World Walker's Water Web is about getting in and serving not just humankind but all kind, graciously aiding all breathing and non-breathing.)

Widening Our Circle

A drop of water on a pond creates a single ripple; in turn, that single ripple causes a second ripple. The second ripple is larger, not smaller, than the first ripple. Perfectly circular, the second ripple creates a third ripple. This unfolding continues until the circles become larger and larger, returning to you. Water is speaking to the world, saying, "This is how it works." It starts with you and returns to you. Who is more important, the smallest ripple circle or the largest? Both!

Water is also teaching teachers how to be unteachers, so that the entire story is expressed. Every individual cell reflects the cosmos, which is you. Are you the beginning of the story or the end? Is the cosmos the beginning of the story or the end of the story? Is this Universe shrinking or expanding, or both?

Water is also teaching teachers how to be unteachers, so that the entire story is expressed. Every individual cell reflects the cosmos, which is you.

We as human beings are part of the entire universe while the universe lives inside our every atom. Long ago we created a false construct that holds time and space to help us organize our experiences and lives; though this construct is limiting. Until now, humans have experienced their existence as something separate from the rest of creation, thus isolating themselves from everything else that lives. This is a delusion indeed, one that restricts us from communing with and influencing all of nature and all nations.

To see the role we as responsible individuals play within the World Walker's Water Web is to acknowledge that we are reflections of the Universal process. We are reflections of all sea gods and their powers. We are to tap into the water only for wisdom. All flowing water and standing bodies of water, such as ponds and lakes, are divided into many layers that move against one another, constantly creating vortices or spirals. It is vortex energy that enables salmon to swim upstream, bees the ability to fly, galaxies to form, and life to be created.

Wisdom is found in these vortices. Manifestation is created within vortices. Hidden wisdom is kept within the "water vortex." The water vortex may hold the secret source of all knowledge and existence. It shows the map of us, and the Universal Mechanism, through picture, sound, and touch. Our oceans respond to the rhythm of the cosmos through the "world vortex."

Who Is a Water Priestess Resources

Meditation #1

Water Sources

Ponder the following while in meditation:

Every water source has its own energies and frequencies with which to work. Every water source's energy changes, depending on the time of day, night, weather, or season. Water makes it very easy for us to work with her energies; only an open heart is needed, and she will fill it to overflowing. Even when troubles come, she is there to make everything crystal clear on how to move through the waters.

You have heard of the column of light; this is the column of water. Water does travel vertically, as well. There are many interesting bodies of water to claim and with which to work, including every form of liquid within our bodies—sweat, saliva, blood, tears, and so on. We are a veritable waterworks!

Meditation #2

While in meditation, move gently (and sometimes not so gently) downstream, not fighting upstream. Repeat to yourself, "I release and choose to move, ever changing." There is one source, and that is the cosmic mind that is within you—is you. You either believe it or not.

If you believe it, then continue to move away from linear thinking, moving closer to your completeness, your fullness, your Higher Self. Not believing changes nothing;

you still remain Goddess's expression of her deep love for you, remaining within her. Begin seeing yourself with no skin costume; begin to see your Self as ever-flowing water. Then witness all you touch.

Common Questions for a Sea Priestess

How does the Water Web work?

It works through water, living streams that reach everywhere in every direction, in every time, using a single vortex. "How" is never important to us.

Who first set up the Water Web?

I was told that it was set up by the Universe, in the beginning, by us. The Water Web was discovered approximately 400,000 years ago by an ancient island city, as a communication network to everything, as well as a mode to travel and a healing and teaching tool. It is sometimes called the "Bridge" or the "Rainbow Bridge." This knowledge was passed on through meditation, dreams, drawings, and dance to the "third root race" and continues to be passed down the same way. I was also told that one must approach the Web with a "pure heart."

How did you find out about the Water Web?

I was instructed by two Root Women to meditate on the ocean for many years. In those seven years of meditation, one of my discoveries was the Water Web. I told them what I saw, and they requested that I explore it and in the right time share it with others like us. I have personally explored and worked with this Water Web since 1962. I now share the Water Web with the World Walkers of the Correllian

Tradition, within the House of Water, and share everything I have found while working with its many light/water streams, crystal seeds, and Healing Stations. The Water Web does not need to be maintained, it maintains us; no new streams need to be created, it creates new streams within itself and us.

Do other traditions use the Water Web?

Yes and no. When working within the Web, no one wears a tradition/religion or dogma patch; it may be utilized by the pure open heart. There are no traditions there, just us. We are vapor, mist, smoke, trade winds, and streams of light, not in human form. We are those who were before we had skin. I do not know how many people on this plane know about this Water Web; I do know I am not the only one who works there.

Now I present this to the precious Correllian shaman because I see no difference between the World Walker and the Correllian shaman. And I share this with the wider world so that everyone may embrace the light of the Goddess through this Water Web.

Exercise #1

Can you find the Water Web? Have fun! No directions are needed; you instinctually know where to find your water. This exercise is about trusting yourself to know that you do know how to enter into the Water Web.

✦ 11 ✦

The Cracked Water Pot

The soul would have no rainbows if the eyes had no tears.
—Native American proverb

Many lands that are now above water were once underwater; likewise, many long-submerged lands used to be above water. More than half of North America once was underwater. Geographical changes have always taken place, rising and falling through time. The second-oldest living, breathing thing in the world is a giant redwood tree, which is at least three thousand years old. The oldest living, breathing thing is the ancient ocean.

The ocean has risen much higher and fallen lower than humankind can imagine, giving land for hundreds of thousands years, then taking it back into itself. Many explorations have proven that there was once more land above the ocean. Many warm islands in the Pacific and Atlantic were once the very top of snowy mountains, indicating long-submerged continents. Cultures rose up for hundreds of thousands of years; then some slowly faded away, while others were swept away in one fell swoop. But if one compares humankind's written history to the entire existence of this world, it is but a tiny speck in relation to all that has taken place in the terrain. No matter how or why they ended, they all ended up under the water.

Some large land masses return to the water, while other land masses return to the many huge world caves within the earth; spaces big enough to fit a large continent. I know in my heart that scientists will find at least one of these spaces in my lifetime; but if not mine, then yours. This is not so far-fetched! I think it will be found on the west coast of North America. For so many years, North America's west coast was thought to be a "new land," but in reality it is one of the oldest lands in the world. Continents also move. Where do you think they are heading? That's right—the water.

The planet earth evolves. Remember that once, as a world people, we were much more evolved. Some races existed for hundreds of thousands of years; compared to them, no nation comes close to the amount of time they spent above the water. They chose to go; when they "died," they chose to stop breathing.

There are wonderful safeguards for experiencing evolved energies; the first is to see yourself as what you really are: love. For most of us, we get split-second flashes; while others can look into the Goddess's eyes of light, using their third eye, or the "bump over their eyes." When you sense what is right next to you and even what resides within you, that sense can be explored by your third eye. Just think of the long-forgotten cultures of the past. It is exciting that there is much more to know! Removing old outdated belief systems is healthy; yet your new knowledge may be as ancient as the ocean.

Cracked Pot Resources

Meditation #1

Begin by sensing and feeling the earth's breath; it breathes as you do. In every breath is knowledge and life. With every breath you take, reclaim your fullness, your will.

As you meditate, enter the silence of your soul, where the fullness of your real Self connects to the Divinity within and without. Feel the connection to the farthest star, because you are just as much there as you are here on this plane.

Meditation #2

It is interesting that science has established the similarities between blood plasma and seawater, confirming our salty past and connection to the sea. Magic, love, and water are the underlying cores and reasons for existing. A simple truth but nevertheless a vast cosmic truth.

Through knowing your own worth comes the memory of who you really are and who you were, formed in the likeness of the ocean. The distant conch shell is blowing, saying, "All love and wisdom are in us all." Dare to reclaim the sacred ground that is you. Such is the illusion of time: gone in a twinkling of an eye. Here on the island, the crossroads of the space/time continuum pass through the thresholds to other realities. Splash!

Exercise #1

Prepare a beautiful place for yourself. Add all the things you love and things that represent you to an altar. Spend a delightful thirty minutes reading and singing the Covenant of the Sea Priestess (found at the back of this book), then sing your song.

Do not take this covenant lightly, because as you speak this sacred text, it is transforming you and your world. It will place a crystal seed over your eyes, causing you to become more aware of your senses, your ever-expansive consciousness, and your very core will slowly change and shine brighter.

Exercise #2

Dream about the Sea Priestesses and allow them to take you on journeys while you sleep and while you meditate. Your initiation night is fast approaching; it is time to ready yourself by dreaming.

12

Falling into the Others

Divine Mind is the one and only reality.

—Charles Fullmore

Scientists are rediscovering the presence of water in our solar system. In 2008, positive signs of water were discovered on Mars in the form of ice. In 2006, the scientific community found a new moon that is completely covered by ice.

Sea Priestesses for hundreds of thousands of years have known that all galaxies float on a vast ocean that connects every system, an ocean of clouds all holding separate galaxies. Sea Priestesses have traveled to the Rainbow Cloud that surrounds this galaxy, and all other galaxies. Scientists call this cloud (our Rainbow Cloud) the Oort cloud, and it is a five-billion-year-old, huge, watery expanse made up of trillions of ice comets.

The Submillimeter Wave Astronomy Satellite was launched in 1998; it detected waves emitted by water everywhere in space. This satellite supports the existence of the Oort cloud. Some scientists believe this cloud formed all earth's oceans, rivers, and lakes by casting thousands of Oort comets toward our precious blue planet.

The Hale-Bopp comet, which last passed through our solar system in 1997, revealed the chemical precursors for life, as reported by Dr. Dale Cruik at NASA's Ames Research Center. Louis Frank of the University of Iowa believes that water did not begin here but landed on earth in large balls of ice or ice comets from deep outer space. It is a fact that mini comets that are composed of water and ice fall into the earth's atmosphere at the rate of ten million per year. These huge snowballs are pulled into our atmosphere, turned into gas, then the gas particles mix with our air and fall to the ground and into bodies of water as rain or snow. Frank reports that as many as twenty comet-like snowballs, measuring as much as thirty feet in diameter, bombard earth's atmosphere every single minute; there they break up into water and dust and fall to the earth as rain or, more specifically, cosmic rain.

In 1998, a new meteorite crashed to earth in Monahaus, Texas. Scientists were amazed to find saltwater when they cracked the meteorite open. It's no surprise that seawater contains all elements known to humankind.

In 1984, the Goddard Space Center found molecules in the beginning stages of organic formation, composed of atoms that are found in living tissue, in interstellar space. Therefore, if water comes from space, and we come from water, does that make us alien to this planet?

All of our selves are connected to these deep-space clouds as well as all water everywhere. As we explore, and as we express our true soul, we will find other selves that are a part of our soul being expressed in other forms, other creatures, other beings, other places. Once you discover your first "other," your heart will leap in astonished joy. You will ask yourself, "What kind of Goddess/God creates a single being that expresses itself with such complexity, such completeness, and allows us to meet many types of species from everywhere, even deep space, through water?" Water is the incubator, the road, and the recorder.

This is the time to step away from your trained mind and enter cosmic rain; step into your full Self, with a capital "S." This may be a little nerve-wracking for some, to purposely lay down everything this culture has taught and pick up what is rightfully ours (even if it's just for a few minutes at a time). We cannot hold both within our hands. You must decide to experience other dimensions by approaching all new thoughts with open, emptied hands.

Stillness without thought will lead you to the genuine you, your gift, your promise. There must be a fully conscious, firm decision to lay down all natural/cultural learning methods to receive "other" information. Remember, you were trained as to what you see and what you don't. I challenge you to consider this awaking to self, to soul, to creation. Setting aside every trained thought, trained perception, just for one moment—this moment—will help propel you forward to the "tipping point," the point where a person is completely willing to dive into the cosmic pool, to dive into the "others'" gifts that have been trained out of us, willing to fall as the comets and seeds are so willing to do.

It will be very difficult for many to isolate into stillness and say to your Self, "I choose to receive information about my Self." Many of us like what we know and how we learned it; if that is the case, then this unteaching is not for you at this point in time. But then again, what brought you here to read these words?

Falling into the Others

Feel Your Self-Desire

"I desire to see my other selves. I desire to become what I was and am becoming." Decide to learn from all your receivers. There are more receivers that we need to reclaim. Decide to hear without ears, see without eyes, and know without trained thought. Decide to learn in a new way, or should I say the first way. Soon, many wonderful Selves will make themselves known to you. Just by making that desire known, your other Selves will begin to make themselves known.

My first experience was when the Root Women said, "Go to the sandy inlet and wait for you." I had no idea what they meant, but as I entered the waters, I knew what I needed to do: float and wait for a big fish to come to me; I would know what to do next. I floated on this little inlet for months, until one day, I finally allowed myself to fall into my Self, to let go. I had to let all words go, let all thought go. In that split second, I heard a rushing and felt movement around me. At the same split second, I received strong communication from the movement of the water.

It said without words, "I am you!" I quickly looked under the water, then jumped out of the sea and ran to the Root Women. I excitedly told them what the water had said to me.

They asked if I had looked under the water to see what had caused the movement, and I said, "Yes, it was a dolphin, a huge dolphin!"

They then asked, "Do you know what you are?"

I said, "Yes."

Then they said, "Sing this in your way: *Waiho wale Kahiko*. This is an ancient proverb that means 'Ancient secrets are now revealed.'"

This was the beginning of self-discovery for me, the beginning of becoming aware of how my soul operates, moves, creates, and has many lives through "others." As I traveled the world I met many of my Selves, from a woman sitting on the ground making baskets to a whale dancing in front of me while I sat on a beach. Every assignment was profoundly simple, but nevertheless brought great fruit and growth. We will find our "others," both macro and micro, from the smallest speck of sand on the beach to the most distant star.

The soul is made of many different beings/places, energies within every dimension. Some beings grow as slowly as coral on the ocean floor or as quickly as beings that move between planets in a twinkling of an eye. We are without form, we breathe and we don't breathe. We fly, we swim, we rise up in curling smoke. We are different within each dimension. We are multidimensional, within multidimensions.

There are many ways to discover our others; some will be presented within the exercise section. The biggest beginning is letting our self let go and allowing our Self to emerge in all their/its/our fullness. Shake off what has hindered desire, and walk in your fullness, your completeness, your promise. Those who struggle with this concept the most are overly tied to all things physical, always thinking of the past, trapped in the physical.

As always, this is the way I was taught; that does not mean it is the only method, just *a* method. I would be told to "do" something, and I would do it until the experience revealed its lesson to me. Then I would go to the Root Women and say, "I learned . . ."

They, in turn, would say, "Good, now what are you going to do with that information?" Or they would just say, "Good." Or they would say, "Go continue doing that until things become clearer for you." Or they would simply say, "Thank you."

This was the most intriguing to me. Why did they say "thank you"? The Root Women would say, "We are not your teacher, the experience is your teacher, you are the teacher."

There were also times when they said nothing. They gave me minimal information; I was the one to experience the information and bring it back to them. Every lesson was reduced to its simplest form to ensure the "trained mind" would stay out of the process. The trained natural mind throws up a thick blanket between all "others" we are interacting with every moment, covering all our senses and hiding some senses completely.

Just by doing all the previous exercises in earnest, you might be experiencing many new unthoughts, new friends, or more of an awareness of what is around you—even your hidden talents. By being more aware of water, one becomes more aware of Self. You will have a strong urge to find your original "free will," your original home, and, yes, the others.

Falling into the Others Resources

Meditation #1

>   Fall within me.
>
>   I have placed within you all my gifts, so that you may place them into our Great Work.
>
>   I have placed all my gifts within you, because it has taken eons to create you.

I am unteaching you to read the words but experience what is being expressed between the words.

Between the thoughts.

I am not teaching your trained brain, I am revealing your soul and all its lighted facets, which have many minds.

Listen with your third eye.

The mind is your greatest asset and your biggest block.

Meditation #2
Healing Will Continue until It's Done

Joining the Healing Stations on the Water Web is most beneficial. As Sea Priestesses/Priests, we are completely equipped to enter the Healing Stations. There is no judgment there, no high nor low, no end.

The following Healing Stations have been in operation for millions of years, started by the first two root races.

1. "Research Station" is for just that, research and for helping all positive scientists discover all things hidden to them. As World Walkers, we are their support system, their muse.

2. "Mind Station" is for healing the mind and exposing the mind to the being, so that the being may see other dimensions.

3. "Soul Station" helps one move to a higher vibration on the grid, exploring other souls in a safe fashion.

4. "Planet Station" is where beings gather to pray for our ill earth, as well as other planets that need healing.

5. "Peace Station" is where beings from all dimensions and planets gather to speak peace into existence by sending light and higher frequencies into all warring planets and nations.

6. "Body Healing Station" is for healing and cleansing bodies.

7. "Rest Station" is for beings to take a break and be cared for.

From all these Stations great inventions have been discovered, stars and planets have been made! To travel to any of these Healing Stations, follow the Water Web to each Station. It is amazingly fun to visit these places, and soon you will find that you love coming to join in with the Great Work.

You will love visiting Mt. Shasta as the white mist rises from beneath the mountain, while all the lovely beings chant and sing for all the parallel earths and stars. It is a celestial blessing to take part in praying for our earth or souls, to stand and say, "Here I am; may I serve?"

Everything is vibration and everything emits sound (which is just another form of vibration). Sound is recorded by the master listener—water—recording everything. Water picks up unique wavelength frequencies from everything, while water emits a sound itself. It is both a receiver and communicator—like us.

Common Questions for a Sea Priestess

What if I am not close to an ocean to do my meditations?

> The soul will always place you next to water. Remember, you have already created a beautiful water temple within your own home. Or you may go astrally to the ocean or another body of water. But then again, there is no other body, because every body of water is connected, thus there is one World Ocean, one universal ocean.

Question: Why is untraining important?

> We have been trained to see only the physical. There is more than what we have been trained to see, hear, and think. To regain the cosmic mind that is rightfully ours, we must untrain our minds. Our natural minds are important to function within this plane and will help us learn many wonderful concepts. There is so much more learning inside and outside this physical reality plane, and, as humans, it is possible to learn all these lessons.

Exercise #1

When you wake up in the middle of the night, ask yourself, "What energies am I sensing within this stillness of the night?" Continue paying attention when you wake up in the middle of the night and journal what you discover.

≈ 13 ≈

The Unteacher

What you resist persists.

—Carl Jung

Teaching is a sacred act; teaching is one of the most underappreciated jobs a person can perform. Many students will never see how much work, study, and meditation enter into preparing a spiritual lesson. A good teacher never shows their students what goes on behind the scenes; their only concern is raising their students up, not the other way around.

A good teacher finds out what the student knows, using that information as a springboard for their lessons. Good teachers wait for the "questions," and only then answer specific questions with great loving care. Answering in such a way as to cause a student to ask more questions ensures that the student is propelled forward to ask even more questions. One must be an explorer to be a good teacher, always learning directly from the living stream in the astral realm and this realm.

To unteach, we lead students to multilevel knowing, moving into other dimension systems, through water, so that students may have the opportunity to see who they really are. Unteaching causes our self to look at realities that will soon be of no use to us and other realities that are now being birthed within this moment. When we move beyond our "trained within an inch of its life" mind, and when we can move beyond this reality system we have created, we then can see that there are no artificial barriers hindering us except those we construct with our own hands. We begin to release anything that holds us back from our journey.

We need to use our abilities, we need to dream big and have big aspirations, so that the entire world will be touched. In fact, even if we dream small, the entire earth participates and changes; the entirety of humankind knows of our dreams and rejoices. The paintbrush is in our hand; it has always been there. The pen has always been there in our hand. Our story is waiting for us to write the next chapter!

To be an unteacher requires patience; not everyone will be willing to listen, but an unteacher does not need to convince anyone. Some truths are not easily accepted. That's why meditation and dreaming are so important to us; those tools help us open to complicated precepts more easily and to dive into the deep sea to experience our lessons.

Unteaching goes on within most dimensions. If you are considering being an unteacher within this reality, here are some concepts to consider.

Teaching on Multilevels

When teaching, we must become more aware of people by watching and listening to what they are revealing to us. Ask them questions and be interested in what they know. Ask them to consider different ways to approach their studies and belief systems. Find out what they desire to learn, not just what you want to teach. You will then touch everyone's hearts, sharing possibilities and introducing many ways to explore other dimensions.

We are now in the days that other realities or levels are willing to show themselves much more easily than in the "past." Many levels are allowing us to take a peek. It is then our responsibility to do the work by dreaming, astral traveling, or meditation work. I am not talking about years of work. The worlds are open to us to step through the gate and experience firsthand what this amazing Universe desires to show us now. The Universe is presenting new and forgotten concepts. It is you who does the dream work to move into the living stream so that you will gain firsthand experience and directions to the next step.

Teaching Others to Connect to the World Ocean

Everything starts with integrity. Start by stating with a pure heart, "I desire to first explore then work within the World Ocean." The water will hear you and answer you, saying, "Enter if you will, if you are able; enter, mystic!" It takes much focused energy to move from the World Walker's Water Web and enter the World Ocean, but you are already here. Desire is the key! Focus turns the key.

If you are a lucid dreamer or astral traveler or can enter meditation without using your mundane mind, you are completely equipped to enter the World Ocean. This is not a privilege held back for only a special group! Some people have made this leap of consciousness ridiculously overcomplicated and untouchable, but it doesn't need to be. You are able to see, because you have spiritual eyes! Your eyes see more than you think!

Assisting Newly Transitioned Beings

This subject of how to assist newly transitioned beings is found within many places, including the astral plane. After meditating in water, you will notice many more precepts written within these lessons, within the mere words, between the lines, between the words. The holy and sacred instructions will reveal themselves to you. If you have been doing the work, everything is within your hands.

The two Root Women would say, "Some 'things' are too sacred to be uttered with a tongue or written with a pen; it is like throwing pearls in vinegar." (Pearls dissolve in vinegar!) Many holy directions are in clear view, in front of your eyes, floating on the quiet surface for you to enter. Nothing is hidden to those of the water.

A good first step is to feel the newly transitioned energy; by feeling for them, you will know where they are located. Then go "there" by willing it and continue to feel how they are transitioning. What are they expecting? Here is the fun part; sometimes you become an actor, whereby you need to be what the newly transitioned needs you to be.

Maybe the person thinks he needs to fight a dragon before he is worthy to enter, so you become that dragon. Or let's say he needs to cross a certain river before entering; then you become the river. You have many choices, and you always have help within this reality system to be what you desire and guidance as to how you can help the newly transitioned beings. With this information, when you have time, go back and reread all these lessons and see what you shall see! After a while, the newly transitioned being will understand they did not go anywhere, but they have the same consciousness and things are much more clear once they wake up.

Setting Up Your Own "Great Healing Center"

After visiting the Great Healing Center that I have introduced to you, you may want to work within this center. All you need to do is be at peace with your Self, and everyone will come to you for your loving training. Start by saying to yourself, "I stand within this access point, within this moment, within this power point, and I access this Great and Holy Healing Center!"

You will then be swept away by loving beings and placed on the crystal rooftop. When you are ready, you may enter and begin to be a student or teacher! There you will remember many things and help birth a new race!

Leading "Planet Healing" Sessions

Every moment I close my eyes, I go to the continuous song that is sung every moment of every second—one song, running through many realities that are all holding this blue planet up, until the illusions are swept away, in unison, bringing this reality back to full health.

To lead a healing session here, within this reality, gather people into a dark room. Ask those around you, "What does this planet need to be healed? What do you need to be healed?" Each person should whisper, one by one, all healings that need to take place within this planet. Ask everyone to remain still for one minute.

Then you will say, "The Holy Ones request that you enter their song by singing your requests to Goddess/God, first one by one, then together." So it's one minute of quiet, one minute of singing requests. After everyone has sung their individual requests, everyone sings together their own chant, their own song, together. As they all sing together, they will begin to sing the song that is sung every moment of every second. Everyone's part of the song will be different. It takes a tremendous amount of loving, higher-frequency energy to do this; however, it can be done if everyone is willing.

The Unteacher Resources

Meditation #1

Entering the House of Water Temple

Follow these steps during your meditation to enter the House of Water temple:

1. Enter the World Walker's temple; light your candle on the altar.

2. After a few minutes of reflection, you will notice a soft blue-green light in the distance behind the altar. Walk around the altar to find a beautiful blue-green pool.

3. Approach the pool and sit along the raised sides of it.

4. Wait for a huge crystal fountain to emerge from the water's placid surface. This fountain will only emerge every once in a while. It will remain above the water's surface for a few minutes, then slowly submerge once again into the deep.

5. When you are ready, you may enter the pool. You can enter the World Ocean from this pool, or you may enter and discover all the wonderful treasures that are waiting for you in the pool to be utilized and used with honor.

6. Here you will meet many friends.

7. Explore or rest. (While resting, the Holy Ones will minister to your every need.) This is where I go to receive my mutterings and many of my teachings; so can you. Every breath you take communicates to the very edge of your Universe and beyond.

Meditation #2

Meditate on the following prompts:

> Through everything, you are able to enter the Holy of Holies and know of their teachings and guidance.
>
> You are both creator and created.
>
> You are broken.
>
> You are complete.
>
> You are a multidimensional being, living in many realities within this moment.
>
> You are I Am; there is no reason to place another word behind I Am.
>
> You are perfect.
>
> You are full of grace.
>
> You have no beginning.
>
> You are limitless.
>
> You are all knowing.
>
> You are the void.
>
> You are everything.
>
> You are everywhere.
>
> You are safe.

You communicate with everything, every time, and every place.

You selected your mother to enter this place.

You are both the mother and daughter of Source.

You are both the father and son of Source.

You are utterly beautiful.

You cannot be contained for long.

You create your story in this time and space construct.

You decided to get on this ride.

You have the capability to change your ride.

You are greatness.

You are the smallest creature.

You are the world's hope.

You have all knowledge.

You are the block and the block remover.

You are the answer.

You limit you.

You are the light and the dark.

You are always exploring distant shores.

You are always dreaming.

You are pure joy and know how to cry.

You are ever changing.

You have no end.

You are forever.

You are bigger than your skin suit.

You decided to be, and so it is!

You decided to experience this reality, and so you are.

As you read these words, feel them sink into your being; allow them to fill you, then see these energies overflow from you.

Do not allow a big ego to develop; though eternity's opening and the entrance to the Holy of Holies is always open, it is the big ego that cannot fit through.

Know there is so much to bring back, and it can only be brought back by you. That is how important you are; that is how important humanity is to this giant experiment.

If a concept is too heavy for you or you feel you are not ready for a particular aspect of the higher energies, know you must do what feels comfortable to you. Some energies are not spiritual; however, they give to the tradition and the Universe in many valued ways. A spiritually minded person is equal to and can learn much from the "this Reality-practical person." So I want you to relax and feel your way through this process. Whatever type of unteacher you decide to be will be just what the Universe needs.

Meditation #3
Nothing Shall Enter
Meditate on the following:

There is a place that awaits.

For all those of the living water.

A temple designed by no hands is waiting for you.

Do you hear the Sea Priestesses singing your ancient name?

Do you hear your heart beating in unison with theirs?

Meditation #4

The Agreement

There was a time when the moon, sun, and ocean agreed to reveal who we are, because they knew many of us have forgotten who we were/are.

The sun said, "When I rise high in the sky, I will throw light upon the water so that humanity may see who they are."

The moon said, "I, too, will do the same; when I rise high in the sky, I will send my light onto the sea so that humanity may see they are stars."

The ocean said, "I will reflect what you send me and touch them, but one question must be asked of all of us. Sun, are you a revelation?"

The sun answered, "Maybe."

The ocean asked the moon, "Are you a revelation?"

The moon answered, "Maybe."

Then the moon and sun asked the sea, "Are you the revelation?"

The sea answered, "Maybe."

Then all three—the sun, moon, and ocean—asked humanity, "Are you the revelation?"

And we said, "Yes."

Common Questions for a Sea Priestess

Why did I need to wait to enter the House of Water temple?

> One must first see they are sacred water before they are able to explore the pool.

Exercise #1

Get a three-ring binder and begin collecting pictures of every form of water. You will be shocked at how many forms water takes! Within every form, the water is speaking to our species. Meditate with these pictures. Be with these pictures, and water will speak to you, because you are indeed a vessel of water! It is always good to keep notes of your explorations.

≈ 14 ≈

Some Water Associations

All knowledge is not taught in the same school.
—Hawaiian proverb

The sea is the home of many well-known and secret gods and goddesses; they live in hidden coral caves or in huge lava tubes deep within the ocean. Some live on the upper portion of the sea, while others live deep on the sea floor. To discover sea goddesses and gods is to be in a cocreator relationship with them for both simple, natural magic and global transformation.

Energies that we can plug into through water gods and goddesses are healing energy, love energy, reflective energy, psychic energy, purification energy, and wisdom. All are available to us as cocreators with the sea. There is a sea goddess and god living within you! Every culture has their water gods, spirits, and associations. The following are just a smattering.

The Sea Goddess

In many temples, the Goddess is represented by a simple bowl of water, the life-giving substance and purifier of mind, body, and spirit.

Types of Energy: Reflective energy, psychic energy, purification energy, and ancient wisdom are available to us as cocreators with the sea through the Goddess. We are a combination of sun energy expressed by the Goddess and all the deep waters she controls. The Sea Priestess is hero, the invisible creator, both gentle and full of strength. However, past cultures and cultures of today neglect her part in humankind's growth, marginalizing anything female. Our records in history are written on every lighted human and with a much more lasting record—our very DNA.

Colors: Blue, green, all colors, or clear (which is not a color).

Magical Tools: The cup, the cauldron, and the mirror are a few examples; however, anything related to water can become a water tool.

Metals: The metals that are usually associated with water are silver, copper, and mercury.

Stones: All transparent or translucent stones; for example, moonstones, amethyst, aquamarine, blue tourmaline, and all clear crystals. Plus, of course, all stones and tumbled glass found in or near living water. There are too many to cite here.

Water Herbs: Kelp/seaweed can be used for all purification rites. An example of a great seaweed is Limu Palahalaha (sea lettuce), which is made of branching, long green blades. It grows on rocks in brackish water. All aquatic plants, water lilies, and the lotus are the Sea Priessess's herbs and decorations. The lotus flower loves the water, so it lives under the water at night; however, it also loves the sun, so it lives above the water during the day. All succulents are water based and can be used for any love, healing, or success rite.

Cleansing: Freshwater or saltwater may be used for tool cleansing, ritual purification baths, and casting a circle.

Water Creatures: All creatures that live in or near the water are spiritual totems for the Sea Priestess. Some examples are: dolphins, sea horses, starfish, seals, sea lions, whales, pelicans, sea gulls, otters, fish, lizards, frogs, snakes, turtles, crocodiles, and alligators to name a few. All these beings serving as living teachers.

Water Spirits

Aside from the Sea Goddess, there are also many water spirits who dwell in the sea and other bodies of water. Water spirits live in all water, and water lives in water spirits. Some examples of these water spirits are:

Oceanides: These are sometimes called ocean nymphs or Salmacis, after the mythological Greek naiad.

Salamanders: As fire elementals, they enjoy residing above or near water.

Undines: These are water elementals. They can also be seen as water nymphs or mermaids. Undines appear to humans in human shape, as well. Undines love human beings and desire to form close relationships with all who invoke and give offerings to them.

Naiads: These are cousins of the water nymphs and are known for their healing powers.

Sirens: Depending on who is talking about these creatures, they can be monsters or fabulous beasts. Sometimes sirens would conjure up fairy sea mist to confuse sailors. They could sense if sailors were about to die and would assist and comfort them as they took their last breaths. Then the sirens would gently guide the sailors to the other side.

Merfolk: The ocean is a landscape where many sea creatures and merfolk live. The main purpose for merfolk throughout the ages is to heal and regenerate a person's mind, body, and spirit. They take care of all the worlds and everyone. They are pure wisdom and love; they provide peace for all.

Water Fairies: They are found in wells, waterfalls, and springs—any source of living, healthy water.

River Spirits: These spirits rule affairs of the heart.

Humans: The most well-known sea creatures are human beings.

We Change Water

We change water so that we can assume the reverse, that water changes us and communicates with us. For several years, a scientist named Dr. Masaru Emoto photographed crystal formations in frozen water after having wrapped the water with a paper that had a positive message, such as thank you, written on it. The water formed perfect crystals.

However, when negative statements were wrapped around the water, the photos would reveal imperfect crystals. Dr. Emoto's research stresses the importance that water has in our lives, individually as well as collectively. The notion that human consciousness affects water, and water reflects our intent, shows how the Universe communicates and creates within itself. He proposes that since humans are made of water, positive messages of harmony will help bring about peace!

This concept that we as humans can move to a higher vibration through water is to say that we are fully prepared to work with water. I highly suggest checking out Dr. Emoto's photos, either in his books or via the Internet. Meditate on the images of the water crystals and see what arises for you!

Stone Lava

Some say Hawaiian park rangers created the "Pele Curse." The Pele Curse states that if you remove a piece of lava from the islands, you are in big trouble with the Goddess Pele; she will hunt you down until you return her rock! Supposedly, by making up this story, park rangers hoped that people would keep their mitts off the lava rocks. Instead, the Hawaiian post office is sent mountains of lava from the mainland every year, because tourists decide to return their rocks to the islands if they felt that the rocks were giving them "bad luck."

If you think lava rocks are bad luck, they are; if you think they are wonderful, they are. I am not advocating removing lava rocks from Hawaii; however, if a lava rock ends up in your possession, consider yourself blessed beyond measure.

The Purple Bump

In a dream, I was told that the water ancients had a soft "purple bump" on their forehead. This bump was and is their third eye. The third eye became less active as cultures moved away from spirit and nature, as people placed more emphasis on physicality and caused entities to focus on what is touched or seen only.

Humankind placed themselves in a tiny box and said to themselves, now let's explore the box, let's write books about the box, let's start religions and worship the box. Let's divide the box and start wars over locations inside the box. Experts in every arena were all giving explanations why it is important to believe in this box. Some taught a one-sided history of the box.

We are not just physical; we know more than what we see with our eyes; we receive with more than just our brain; we are more. We have more than one mind within our bodies, yet we are part of one mind. We are bigger than our physical body and hear farther than we can with just our ears.

For a month, decide to open your third eye. See your eye open; touch, smell, see beyond seeing, and say in your own words, "I will allow my purple bump to be what *it* is." Stop thinking and allow your bump to be what it is, not what you think it is. The third eye does more than just see. The third eye has all the senses that reach into all others and all dimensions in all places and time. Experiment by using all your senses through your third eye. Once you have accomplished that task, begin exploring what other senses you remember.

Half Truths

If you already know how to lucid dream, try this exercise.

Before you fall asleep, tell your Higher Self that you want to meet your "water guardians" tonight. As you fall deeper into slumber, go to a favorite sacred body of water. Float and relax, allowing your water guardians to come to you, minister to you, heal you, love you, prepare you, fill you. Meet with them as often as you need to be able to see your face within them. You will experience many wonderful changes. If ever you experience something negative or confusing, then you are not in control. Remember, you are in control; it is your dream! Otherwise, leave that dream state until you are willing to take authority over your dream.

We are not here to judge or make you feel negative in any form. If you experience a negative feeling, you have not broken away from the "trained within an inch of its life" brain. This brain is too busy chattering and giving you many so-called good reasons to learn this lesson later; thus the trained mind has just told you what to do, instead of the other way around.

Yes, you can learn wonderful things and go very far using the trained mind, and that is good; however, one can never experience who they really are until they let go, allowing the World Ocean to love you back to Self, falling into her to heal you back to holy Self. You are more than what your trained mind can ever conceive.

This is the scary part for many. They have been trained that all they are is what they have been trained to believe. We have been trained that we have a single, thinking mind and that we are only solid matter. This is half-truth. The only thing worse than a lie is a half-truth.

Half-truths keep us away from our own free will, our own Higher Self, all our minds, and the "others." There is more within nothing than something.

Calling the Others in Meditation

Within the stillness of meditation, call forth your "others"; call upon all your loved ones, who are all ancestors. As you walk through your day, know you are in a dream and begin to call forth each parallel other, acknowledging they exist and loving them.

Watch for their "in the bottle" messages, meaning that, most of the time, their messages are contained within something else. Your loved ones will communicate with you, or they will bring you to where they live—not showing themselves, yet showing you what you are doing at this eternal moment. Be aware of what you are seeing. Look between the spaces, between each moment. When asking for confirmation, stay alert for the answer, wait for the answer.

Calling the Others while Awake

The next time you see a bubble, from any source (a child blowing a bubble, spraying bubbles from a wave, a drop of dew on a leaf, a raindrop on a window), look at light reflections, colors, and shadows through your eyes and your third eye. Go into trance and discover each world that becomes revealed within each bubble. See, feel, smell, taste, sense, and know.

Water Association Resources

Meditation

Still Waters

Use the following words to guide your meditation:

> I am the source of all manifestation.
>
> Am I telling a story, or is the story telling us?
>
> The strongest currents are under still waters.
>
> The sea of forgetfulness washes away all half-truths to reveal supreme purpose.
>
> Purification will usher in transformation.
>
> Unforgiveness will slow the life flow toward us, rendering water's unlimited resources useless.
>
> Each depth has its own lesson and gift. Drink in the cool, refreshing energies that only water can give, revealing our very soul.
>
> Breath is connected and reveals cosmic consciousness . . . harmony . . .

Float on the water and feel your breath; then, when you are ready, sink below the water (on the astral plane) and feel your breath and your energies interacting with the water energies. Breathe under the water. Sink a few hundred feet below the water's surface and experience those energies interacting with your energies.

Continue to drop thousands of feet below the surface and experience those energies. With each change within the water level, you change.

Continue to travel downward until you reach the ocean's soft floor. Stay there and receive through non-words, gestures, feelings, and seeing the ocean engulfing you completely with all the energies you have collected as you moved to the ocean floor.

Allow all of those energies to take form and take care of your every need. Allow them to prepare you, dress you. When you are ready to move back up to the surface, see yourself moving through all these levels.

Once at the surface, many see they have many more "main" chakras than just the seven or nine that we have been trained to see. Look at your hands with your third eye. Look at your heart. Listen for sounds, feel, see if there is a new energy around you; ask it questions.

It will longingly want you to come back, and you will.

Did an "other" follow you home?

Exercise

The Fool Jar

This exercise was done by thousands of people all over the world as an experiment to prove to themselves that, in fact, water is very reactive to human thoughts and words.

People placed two glass jars of cooked rice in two different places within their home. They then spoke to each jar. To one jar they said, "Thank you." To the other jar, they said, "You fool." They did this for one month.

After one month, the "thank you" jar fermented into a mellow smell of malt. The "fool" jar rotted and turned black. One family took this experiment one step farther and prepared a third jar of rice. They decided to completely ignore this jar. The results were that this third jar rotted faster than the "fool" jar. Your exercise is to consider what this experiment means to you, write it down, and date it. Decide what this assignment means to you.

～ 15 ～

Sea Priestess Initiation

> Man alone is the architect of his destiny. The greatest revolution in our generation is that human beings, by changing the inner attitudes of their minds, can change the outer aspects of their lives.
> —William James

Now it is time to move through your Sea Priestess initiation. If you enter this initiation with your ego, nothing will be revealed. Enter this initiation with a loving, open, humble heart, and all relating to the waters will be revealed every day of your life in the physical plane and beyond into your bridgeless long life.

Instructions

Take a long, refreshing, ritual bath any way you prefer. Adding candles or darkness is up to you. Dress in white, placing a covering over your head.

Repeat the words from the Covenant Chant and the Covenant of a Sea Priestess below. Say these statements as if they are true for you, because they are for you.

The Covenant Chant

I sing.

What is a Sea Priestess?

Who is a Sea Priestess?

What do I do?

How do I speak?

How do I think?

How do I see?

How do I heal?

How do I breathe?

Where do I live?

Everywhere.

Shall I mother the water?

Reveal to me the Sea Priestess temple!

Where is my sea altar?

Where is my sea heart?

Send me my Sea Priestess tools!

As a Sea Priestess, I shall calm the waters!

I will heal all by my free will!

I stand in my fullness.

I sing the song that has sung me into existence, for I am beyond all that I am, for I have already entered eternity!

One

more

time!

Precepts to Consider before Your Covenant Event

We already carry the promise within us, as we are within everything. We are who made us; we are not apart from Source. Source only knows how to create creators; thus we are the creator that creates. Nothing dies. All is ever-expanding consciousness that resides within us as full human. It is we who create every story. It is we who are now creating this multi-Universe's story at this very moment.

We have purity of heart, no judgment on another's perspective. We are not above another; for if we were, we would not be able to remain in the water. We are already whole; we are already worthy to enter the Holy of Holies. We are already at the finish line and so is everyone else!

As you have noticed, you have already been slowly integrating yourself through the previous lessons. As you studied each lesson, you focused on the main subject matter within each it, moved through action-oriented exercises, and activated many parts of your Sea Priestess body through meditation. Now is the timeless time to complete your initiation by reciting the Covenant of a Sea Priestess.

Getting Ready for Your Covenant Experience

It is your choice whether to have music softly playing in the background or incense glowing as you walk through this sacred ritual. You are most welcome to add anything you like to the ritual or dress in any way you prefer. If possible, ask a friend to slowly read the covenant to you.

You will also need:

- a lighted candle, color of your choice, charged with an oil of your choice
- shells (optional)
- a veil
- a printed or handwritten copy of the covenant

Once you have your tools in place, have your friend read the covenant slowly to you. Take many breaks and have your friend give you time to integrate everything that is said.

After the covenant is read, take a moment, then pour wax from your charged candle on the bottom of the sheet of paper on which the covenant is written.

Place your index finger and the reader's index finger into the poured wax so that you leave two fingerprints. This signifies that the holy covenant was sealed and completed.

Following the sealing of the covenant, astrally travel to the Sea Priestesses' temple, and rest within the temple until you feel you are ready to return here within this mundane world.

Because you are filled with joy, you are capable of sharing your abundance. Because you are filled with peace, you are capable of creating peace. Because you are filled with hope, you are capable of sharing hope. Because you are filled with wonder, you are capable of hunting and bringing back the world's treasures. You are a blessed being; go forth and discover what is yours and ours.

Mark this day, for you will never be the same! Blessings shall follow you home.

The Covenant of a Sea Priestess

Every Sea Priestess has many talents, and each talent shows up differently every time. Every Sea Priestess possesses all the following attributes:

- She is a quiet hunter of caves, all bodies of water, treasure, and other Sea Priestesses.
- She is a teacher, turning knowledge right-side up again while uncovering hidden wisdom.
- She is an explorer, a pioneer, offering hope where there is none.
- She creates peace.
- She is a living map of all the supernovas and sees beyond deep space, recognizing more water is out there than in here on this plane.
- She can be found in the smallest dewdrop, on the highest mountain, or below the deepest cave under the sea's floor.
- She sees beyond time while living here.
- A Sea Priestess is a wild wave rider of all oceans, everywhere, on every planet, and in the ocean in which galaxies reside.
- She is an underwater visionary.
- She needs no tools outside herself.
- She walks all worlds and owns the Underworld. We are ministers to all bodies of water everywhere.

- A Sea Priestess needs no religion or doctrine to be guided, nor needs a face on her Source.
- She needs no books, for the water is her teacher. Her books are every creature found in our life.
- She is both sea seed and star dust.
- She is both seed and seeder.
- She is both planter and harvester of animals and plants.
- A Sea Priestess needs no stories, yet creates many beginnings.
- A Sea Priestess understands and is what Goddess is, both female and male energies.
- She does not have compassion; she *is* compassion.
- She possesses and understands both female and male energies/essences. Moving between this deep dream and eternity becomes clear to her.
- She does not possess love; she is strong, limitless love, healing the single soul.
- She uncovers the hidden.
- She delivers hidden treasures on both sides.
- A Sea Priestess moves between this dream and eternity.
- She gently presents the promise from within.
- A Sea Priestess is patient (for the most part).
- A Sea Priestess sees perfection in every living thing.

- A Sea Priestess does not possess love; she *is* love.
- She heals at soul level.
- She is a voyager, traveling often to gain "new/old" information to share with the rest of us.
- She holds knowledge and direction from the multi-universal ocean in a single teardrop.
- She may take refuge in the Holy Temple of the Sea Priestess, a temple that was created before humans decided to explore consciousness in flesh, blood, and bone.
- She searches for the others.
- She is the sea's lighted heart.
- She moves with the waters; she is the morning rain.
- She quietly stays within the waters, helping this great birth.
- She is capable of reading between the words and seeing beyond the flames.
- She influences the flame, the wind, and the soil.
- She has walked a lonely, long road, seeing beyond symbol.
- She sees beyond the ancient chant "I Am," helping souls to find their way home.
- A Sea Priestess has been hurt and has risen from her pain; she sees beyond all.
- She has come close to death and laughed.

- A Sea Priestess is loving, a humbled lover of humanity and all species that have a heart to hear.
- She sees beyond this body symbol, all symbols, to reveal her altar.
- She is always found within the loving arms of the Holy of Holies; she and it are one.
- A Sea Priestess is not afraid to feel the oceans' emotions nor her own.
- She is capable of changing the world while no one is watching.
- She is a healer of all species that have a heart to feel.
- She is eternal, exploring her ancient home.

It is now time to move through the water and show them who they are. Do you feel the ancient fires? Do you feel the depths of the ancient seas affirming what you already are? A Sea Priestess "Is."

Are you able to ask, what am I?

You see beyond this body symbol, all symbols, to find your altar within the arms of the Holy of Holies, in the very center of the Universe, which is you.

It takes courage to enter this high order. We offer a song that can only be heard only by the soul. Because the brightness will reveal every shadow you possess, you must gently deal with your shadows according to your calling and chosen task. Nothing is hidden from you.

You hold an ancient song that can be heard by only your soul and can be sung only by you, a Sea Priestess. We have never harmed a sailor at sea; however, we have helped them cross into eternity. We love them; we do not kill them.

It takes strength to surrender and to release all outward attachments. The next time you see a women walking along the beach who has light in her eyes and a sure step or feel drawn to this person sitting quietly near or on the water, you may be witnessing one of us. If you feel the urge to approach her, please do. Ask her what she knows, even though she may start by saying, "I'm no authority; there are others who are experts in this subject." Listen to the humble-hearted, for they have much to share but will share only when asked. She is unlike the ego-driven person who thinks she knows more than you.

If those words have not pushed you away, then stay and listen to what comes out of your mouth, for they will reveal what you are. Allow your entire being to receive the "knowing," the pearls of wisdom, to be absorbed by your very heart as you return as the pearl of the sea.

It is now time to move through the waters. Do you feel the ancient ocean that this planet floats upon? Do you feel the depths of the ancient seas affirming what you already are? You are a Sea Priestess, lighted by your own heart from within. You ask what is a Sea Priestess. I ask, what are you? As you move into deep waters, everything changes if you allow it by your will and purpose. Do you see the other communications here, speaking to you, telling you the rest of what a Sea Priestess is?

Do you have the capacity to rise from your mind and swim in the Mind of the cosmic ocean and see through a Sea Priestess's eyes? You do have the capacity. By knowing that information, you are forever changed.

For many who are reading or hearing these words, you will have walked lonely roads, experiencing much disappointment; while others may have felt that they have never "fit in," never felt at home. Some have walked through great loss or lived lives that seemed to always miss the mark.

Maybe for the first time in your life, you are beginning to realize that you are coming home; you realize that you have found your way. You are welcome here. After absorbing all these lessons, you will finally exhale and fully breathe in the waters of peace as you are directed to the Holy of Holies. Rest and just be.

You are home. Listen for your song from deep blue, for the rest of us are sending your ancient song from the most distant star sea. Your ocean song! You are love. There is nothing to do but experience this remarkable love. The world is waiting for this pure love through you. Many realities are working with us; others are waiting for us, as we are waiting for others. I seal this with an eternal, Divine kiss on the top of your forehead and on your hands.

I pour liquid candle wax on your fingers. I do the same as we seal this covenant, this day, on this page.

The second part of your initiation is to experience the Sea Priestess coming to you in one of your dreams.

You are a Sea Priestess of the highest order; if you do not believe this, ask for confirmation and it will be given. The fact that we are finally together is our confirmation and witness. You have traveled a long way from home to receive this honor; this honor has always been yours. In the eyes of a Sea Priestess, you shall see eternity. May warm waves sweep over you this bright day; feel the others pouring white liquid stardust across your eyes and within your heart. Drink the water of the Divine. You are a Sea Priestess as you have always been and always will be.

In the water you remain.

We confirm this day, [month/day/year], this covenant of the Sea Priestess to be one with eternity by our mark.
    I confirm by my hand, your hand, and all Sea Priestesses, that you have always been one of us.

Stephanie Leon Neal~
Sea Priestess since 1962

You may now add the wave (~) after your name, indicating your service to the water and all she touches.

What to Do Next

It is up to you. If you continue to live the way you have been, nothing new will come; if you live fully, not being a spectator, you will learn many new concepts firsthand.
    Select all of the suggestions below, or one, or none. Rest assured, becoming an explorer will cause you to be smack in the center of every selected experience.

- Create your own dream dictionary.
- Create your own charts.
- Create your own ritual, for you are a living ritual.
- Creates your own story/life.
- Create your own purpose.
- Create your own meditation.
- Create your own prayers.
- Keep a journal for those who will follow after you.

- Experience, firsthand, all that you desire to learn.
- Go on your own adventure or hunt.

Believe in your own strength, your own power, your own purpose. There is still so much forgotten information; allow it to well up inside. There is an ocean of new information about everything waiting to be uncovered.

Congratulations! It is now your time to change this world one drop at a time.

About the Author

Stephanie Neal was first taught to read the I Ching and the tarot by her mother-in-law, Margaret Neal. She later trained as a Third Degree Cleric within the Correllian Tradition and as a Reiki Master, and she traveled the world, which brought many experiences from the sea.

Her formal education as a Sea Priestess consisted of being taught by two Root Women in Oahu, Hawaii, from the age of twelve to the age of eighteen, and she was initiated in 1965 at age fifteen. Stephanie was then given the task to continue studying throughout her life by visiting as many shorelines as she could, so she did. She has been a Sea Priestess teacher (or unteacher!) ever since.

Under the First Priestess of the Correllian Tradition Krystel High Correll, Stephanie was initiated into the Correllian Tradition as a member in 2003, becoming a first-degree clergy member in 2004 and eventually becoming part of the High Priesthood in 2006.

She is also the founder and head of Sacred Sea Temple, established as a personal shrine in 2004; the appointed head of the World Walkers' Order; and was later appointed by Chancellor Don Lewis High Correll and Arch Priestess Krystel High Correll as First Elder, then as First Priestess of the Correllian Tradition in 2015. She was officially Invested in April 2016.

Stephanie is continually honored to serve the Tradition's tenets and its talented general membership, as well as the profoundly dedicated clergy.

She lives with her gifted husband, Mike, and is also a mother to a remarkable son, Michael, and daughter-in-law, Amy, and grandmother to Chase.

For more information about the Correllian Tradition and to connect with other Sea Priestesses and Priests, please visit us at *www.correllian.com*.

www.ingramcontent.com/pod-product-compliance
Lightning Source LLC
Chambersburg PA
CBHW022101160426
43198CB00008B/308